GARDEN RENOVATION

GARDEN RENOVATION

Transform Your Yard Into the Garden of Your Dreams

Bobbie Schwartz

TIMBER PRESS
PORTLAND, OREGON

Published in 2017 by Timber Press, Inc.

The Haseltine Building
133 S.W. Second Avenue, Suite 450
Portland, Oregon 97204-3527
timberpress.com

Printed in China
Second printing 2018

Cover design by Stacy Wakefield Forte
Text design by Laura Shaw Design

Library of Congress Cataloging-in-Publication Data

Names: Schwartz, Bobbie, author.
Title: Garden renovation: transform your yard into the garden of your
    dreams / Bobbie Schwartz.
Description: Portland, Oregon: Timber Press, 2017. | Includes
    bibliographical references and index.
Identifiers: LCCN 2016055618 | ISBN 9781604696127 (pbk.)
Subjects: LCSH: Gardens—Design. | Gardening.
Classification: LCC SB473 .S398 2017 | DDC 635—dc23 LC record available
    at https://lccn.loc.gov/2016055618

A catalog record for this book is also available from the British Library.

To my loving husband, Niki,
who has always encouraged me,
puts up with my extensive travels,
and never fails to make me smile.

Contents

Foreword

Bobbie Schwartz has been a successful landscape designer for years, specializing in residential design, while also taking on some commercial work. She has judged design contests; she has mentored new designers; and she has been president of the Association of Professional Landscape Designers, not once but twice. Not only does she know how to design, she is an authority on perennial plants. She is also well versed in trees, shrubs, ornamental grasses, and other plant groups. This combination of design knowledge and plants makes her "a keen plantswoman," to quote the British.

One of the major design problems most homeowners face is not planting a blank slate, but rejuvenating an existing garden. They're often faced with a suburban builder's 1940s design across the front yard, or a former homeowner's hodge-podge creation, or an expensive new home with an $80 landscape. These scenarios are all daunting. It's hard to consider either full surgery or multiple amputations. Most people cringe when you tell them they have to pull out a half-dead tree, or that the plant material in their yard is either too small or too big and adds nothing to their house, or that what they do have is planted in the wrong place.

It takes a well-versed, authoritative designer to deliver the dreaded but tactful, magic words: "Perhaps we can find a different place for that plant" (instead of "that plant has to go!"); "Don't you think your visitors would be more comfortable if the path were wider?" (short for, "your path is too narrow"); or words to that effect for any other changes that need to be made.

Gardeners, like everyone else, are reluctant to change. However, logic, along with simple plans and pictures, can enhance your garden makeover, make it a great experience, provide years of enjoyment, and give you some humorous experiences along the way. Take Bobbie's advice and then go for it!

—STEPHANIE COHEN, prize-winning author, national speaker,
and fellow of the Garden Writers of America

Preface

I N MY MANY YEARS AS A GARDENER and certified landscape designer, I have met very few people who are satisfied with their landscapes. I see so many frustrated homeowners who know they want to make changes but have no idea where to start or what questions to ask. And while there are hundreds of books that talk about various aspects of the landscape, few tie them all together in a way that gives you the confidence to embark on such a project. In this book, I hope to give you the knowledge you'll need to begin that journey. The process will leave you with a garden that brings you endless joy and pleasure and a great sense of accomplishment for making a positive change to your surroundings.

This is a very personal book. The process of landscape reinvention can reveal a lot about yourself. You will need to think long and hard about who you are and what your tastes, needs, and wants are in relation to your property. If you fail to do this, your new landscape will not fulfill your aspirations. Landscaping can be just decorative or it can be substantive, a fulfilling extension of your home. Whether you call it renovation or reinvention, the key is acknowledging that you want change in your landscape, that you are no longer willing to accept the ordinary and the common. You want your landscape to make you feel good.

This process may seem overwhelming, but it doesn't have to be if you know which questions to ask. I'll pose many of them for you. Your job, then, will be information gathering, and coming up with the answers. If you divide your landscape into sections and prioritize the order in which you want to change things, the task will not seem as daunting as you think. You will have a plan with a starting point and then successive phases.

We will begin where all successful projects begin: with a focus on your goals and budget. We can then concentrate on evaluating the components of your existing landscape, and suggest ways to enhance what you already have. Finally, we will take a hard look at the plants you have and think about new ones that can be added. As you move from kickoff to touchdown, you will come up with a strategy to balance out the demands of time and money, asking many important questions along the way. How much do you want to tackle yourself? Can you create impact inexpensively? Should you pay for expertise? What are the differences between a landscape designer and a landscape architect? How can you best make use of that expertise?

Writing this book has called on all of the knowledge and experience I've accumulated in my forty-eight years as an obsessed gardener and forty years as a landscape designer. I'm happy to share with you and hope that reading the book will help you achieve your goals. My gardening and design experience has mostly been gathered in zone 6 where I live, but the principles of landscape design are universal. Obviously, if you live in more extreme climates, you will have to substitute plant material that is suitable to your zone, but the basic forms, textures, colors, and sizes can almost always be found in plants that grow well in your region.

There is a wealth of information in other books and online about the many aspects of horticulture and landscape design upon which I have touched only lightly. Take advantage of the bibliography and resources to broaden your understanding of particular subjects in which you are interested.

The principles of landscape design are a starting place but there are no design police who will arrest you if you do not always follow the rules or make up some of your own. Remember that what you create is yours and reflects who you are. So take your time, and have some fun along the way.

Choosing Change

I KNOW EXACTLY WHAT SOME OF YOU ARE FEELING. When we moved into our current house, we were in love with the building itself, but the landscape was a different story. It was the embodiment of the "garden from hell": huge swaths of lawn, aggressive groundcovers everywhere, one bed of white pebbles over black plastic, a dying Chinese elm, three smelly hawthorns, virtually no flowers, and all shrubs pruned into boxes and balls. The only assets were two huge magnolias, a slew of old Japanese pieris (*Pieris japonica*), and a well-designed, but old, concrete patio.

The house we had just left had a huge perennial bed and a delightful redesigned (by me), shady front yard—it was the garden of my dreams. I knew that I had to quickly find a starting point on my new property so that I could begin again to create my new landscape. The starting point turned out to be the pebble-filled bed in the back yard; it was relatively bare and seemed like a manageable space. (What I did not anticipate, however, was the amount of back-breaking labor that would be entailed in digging it out.) I have since labeled that area the right garage bed.

Logically, then, the next area to be renovated was the left garage bed. In the succeeding years, I cleared the magnolia bed (left of the left garage bed) and then the kitchen bed (left of the magnolia bed). After that, I began the task of working on the fence bed

▷ With the exception of the bulbs that I planted the fall before we moved in, this was the original front yard landscaping when we moved into our house.

◁ Even in October, I have lots of color from perennial mums and asters and the yellow foliage of *Hakonechloa macra* 'All Gold' and *Lysimachia nummularia* 'Aurea'.

◁ This area in my back yard, formerly only white pebbles and black plastic, is now filled with a multitude of perennials, grasses, and vines.

▷ Along my driveway, this bed is full of color from spring through fall.

▽ The front hill bed, close to my neighbor's driveway, is predominantly blue and purple.

that adjoined the right garage bed. The entire back property consists of varying degrees of sun and shade but no full sun.

Once I had redesigned the beds in the back, I was ready to tackle the full-sun areas that could only be found in the front of the house. The bed that was there when we moved in was the epitome of outdated landscaping. Our home was built in 1924, a time when most gardeners were European immigrants who still favored the formal pruning style of their former homelands. (They were also cheap.) Since I am most certainly *not* a formal person, I tried to let the constrained shrubs of the foundation planting grow out naturally. This entailed endless hours of pruning in order to keep them in scale with the house. After finally getting overwhelmed with this work, I just ripped them out. I replaced them with a variety of shrubs, grasses, and perennials that were lower maintenance and provided much more beauty and interest as well as habitat for all the other creatures that share the space.

Eventually, I decided that the bed needed to be deepened in order to create more interesting, layered compositions—that was phase two. By that time, I had become a full-fledged plant-a-holic and needed more space for all the plants I wanted to trial. Phase three began within a few years, when I added contiguous beds down the length of my driveway and my neighbor's driveway. That process basically took six years, though I am still constantly tinkering with everything.

A landscape that I once hated has now become one that feels like a beautiful extension of my home. I can hardly wait to go outside each day to see what's changed from the day before. Where I once felt ensconced in rigidity, I now feel as if my bonds have been untied and I can sway in the wind.

Why Renovate?

Before you begin, it is wise to concentrate on the reasons behind your renovation, your goals, and your budget. Important questions await your input. Have you moved into a new house and don't know what you have, how to take care of it, or how to change it? Did you purchase the house in spite of the landscaping? Are the plantings out of scale or poorly sited?

Maybe you have lived in your home for several years with a landscape that was merely acceptable. Perhaps your children are now grown, you've put them through college, and your son or daughter wants to have his or her wedding in your back yard. You may decide that it is time to beautify the back yard in such a way that you will enjoy the space long after the wedding.

When you look out the window or drive down the street, do you envy the landscapes you see elsewhere? Is your landscape tired? My dear friend and fellow gardener Stephanie Cohen always compares foundation plantings from the 20th century to clothing we wore 20 to 30 years ago that we wouldn't dream of wearing now. Does your landscaping have that same feel? Does it have geometrically pruned shrubs in old foundation beds? Does it have beds that don't make sense or are full of plants that aren't doing well?

The landscaping, both softscape (the plants) and hardscape (the paving and structures), might be a mishmash because it was done piecemeal, either at different times, or with different companies or designers. And whether you need to deal with an overgrown or badly planted yard or new landscaping, you still need to know how to edit the garden as it matures. Editing involves pruning, pulling unwanted annual or perennial seedlings as well as volunteers, and transplanting.

COMFORT LEVEL

There are many factors to consider when establishing your plan of attack for renovation. Does your landscape feel comfortable? If not, try to pinpoint why it doesn't. Does it feel claustrophobic? I frequently see homes where the trees—often conifers, but also dense deciduous trees—are planted too close to the house.

Even if you love the mature blue spruce in your front yard, perhaps it's planted in front of some windows and makes the room inside dark and gloomy. Maybe it is also planted so close to the house that the branches now brush against the exterior and the roof, doing gradual damage to both. Do you leave it or remove it (a very expensive proposition)? The tree's color automatically makes it a focal point, but you could keep that aspect by either replanting one further from the house or planting a dwarf cultivar (remembering to allow for mature size).

Frequently, home entryways are flanked by conifers that are too large. They constantly need pruning and can also create a claustrophobic feeling. Depending on their size, it might be possible to transplant them to the outer edges of the front beds.

▷ This is a typical and forbidding foundation planting; a multitude of dark evergreens hide the entrance and windows.

Another factor causing claustrophobia may be shrubs that have never been pruned, thus growing so high above windowsills that the rooms within are very dark. Some shrubs can be renewed by pruning, although that kind of pruning is a job that never ends. Time for a decision: you can keep those shrubs (maintaining a semblance of maturity) and all the work that will entail, or you can replace them with new ones that will never grow tall enough to block out the windows (though you will have to accept living with immature plants for three to five years). These are the kind of debates you will need to have with yourself throughout this process.

△ In this updated landscape, the unusual shingle fence and vine-covered arbor entice and welcome the visitor to the front door.

FEELING WELCOME

Passage to the front door should be welcoming and pleasurable. Think about this as you go in and out of your house. Are there beds parallel with the sidewalk? If not, consider whether the experience would be more pleasurable if there were. If the sidewalk has these beds but feels cramped because the plantings beside it are encroaching on that walking space, maybe the beds need to be deepened and the plantings transplanted further back from the walk.

▷ This house is so hidden by the plantings that you can only see the garage. Where is the front door?

▽ A wide stoop and step are inviting and comfortable—and leave room for decorative containers.

Take note of the experience when approaching the front door. Pretend you're visiting for the first time. Is the path to the door obvious? Quite often, a visitor has to walk up the driveway and then assume that there will be a walkway to the front door even though the walk is hidden from the street.

Are the front steps wide enough, and the stoop deep enough? If you feel as though you are going to fall off the landing when you open the screen or storm door, it might be time to consider a change. How high is the stoop? Perhaps a railing is required. Would a larger stoop and wider stairs be more graceful as well as more comfortable and safer?

USABLE SPACE

One problem that many homeowners face is figuring out what to do with seemingly unusable or ugly space. Many homes have relatively narrow side yards that are merely a means of access from the front to the back of the property and generally devoid of interest. That avenue could become something special if the space were treated as a decorated hallway. The journey through it would be much more interesting if a curvilinear path were constructed rather than a straightforward one. Any material will work, but consideration should be given to echoing one of the materials of the house or other hardscaping.

Frequently, side yards are fenced in with a gated entrance. An ordinary gate that matches the fence would be the cheapest and perhaps easiest option, but expending some creativity on your gate would make the entrance more inviting.

I have seen many creative approaches to the side yard dilemma. The owner of a Chicago home turned one of the side yards into a series of terraced outdoor rooms. Thus, ugly space became a joyful journey from the front yard to the back. Several narrow properties in Newport, Kentucky, were designed with stone paths set between narrow planting beds or between a series of planted containers. These paths serve as journeys to interesting but small back yards.

△ This curvilinear concrete path repeats the use of concrete from the driveway of the home. As the plants on the left mature, the walk will become more enjoyable.

Perhaps you have a lovely patio that you rarely use because it receives too much sun. You might consider building an arbor over it, to which you can add either shade cloth or vines with large foliage that will provide shade.

Perhaps the patio is very shady but its surroundings are bare. Maybe you've procrastinated over making any changes due to a lack of knowledge about shade-loving plants that would be appropriate for the space. Or maybe the existing patio is in poor shape, which is often the case. Should you start from scratch or try to preserve the stone or brick by lifting it and setting it aside, putting down a stable (permeable) base, and then re-laying the stored material? Is the patio large enough? Does it also need to be reconfigured?

▷ This wooden gate immediately attracts the eye while still maintaining the owner's privacy.

◁ Terraced rooms were created at the side of this house with a set of pergolas, steps, and a lattice fence (unseen) to the right.

◁ An irregular cut stone path, bordered by narrow planting beds filled with plants of different textures, leads to the back patio.

▷ When the vines growing on this metal arbor mature, they will shade the patio below.

SCREENING

Do you need to add screening for privacy or perhaps to block the view of something unseemly outside of your property? If you live on a busy street with lots of traffic, one solution could be to build walls that create an inner courtyard with the only visual access to the property being the driveway or the front walk. When you are in your back yard, are you looking at your neighbor's unkempt back yard or even junk cars? How can you screen them out? There are many options, including fencing, panels, and plants. Are your garbage cans or air conditioning units eyesores? Think about ways that they can be disguised or hidden. Also, if you have a hot tub or are thinking of installing one, screening can be used to create additional privacy.

△ The stone patio at the front of the house can be accessed only from the walk to the front door or from the living room.

△ The patio wall that screens the view from the street is constructed of the same stone as the patio fireplace.

△ Clematis climb this lattice fence that was designed to echo the architecture of the house and hide the concrete pad on which the garbage cans are kept.

Increasing Your Home Value

There are innumerable reasons to reinvent your landscape, but an often-overlooked one is that doing so is an investment in your home that will ultimately bear greater returns than the stock market. There have been many studies showing that the value of your home will increase and that it will eventually sell faster if the landscaping is appealing. A 2014 *Wall Street Journal* article reported that a home's value can increase by 7 to 14 percent with an attractive landscape. Other studies, including one from the *Journal of Environmental Horticulture*, show that homes with attractive landscapes can see a 14 to 17 percent increase in sale value over homes with unattractive or plain landscaping. In other words, the initial financial pain of reinventing your landscape will be mitigated by the long-term financial gain. Still, the greatest benefit of all will be the enduring pleasure it brings you.

Defining Your Goals

Defining your goals is a crucial part of any landscape renovation project. If you don't have an idea of what you want out of your garden, your redesign will not have any focus. And sometimes, goals conflict, so it is important to settle those conflicts before you start making changes. What if there's not enough space for a larger patio as well as a large play area for your children? Your goals will direct the design. Think of yourself as the director, and your space as the set. How are you setting the mood before the cast (the plants) arrives?

△ With no definition of back lot lines, these properties blend seamlessly into each other.

Before we get to the various features of your landscape and the ideas you may have for them, we need to start with the basics. First, find your purchase documents. A plat plan (survey document that shows where your lot lines are and what, if any, restrictions or easements apply) should have been included with your closing papers. You must know where your property lines are. If you don't have a plat plan (your city zoning office often has one for your property), consider hiring a surveyor to mark the lines to avoid future disputes with your neighbors. You or your landscape designer will need this plat plan to determine how much space you have and to lay out your garden ideas. In many suburban communities and in rural areas, lot lines are often defined only by survey markers, assuming that they are still there. Many homeowners prefer more defined lines but fences are often prohibited. Think about other ways to define your space.

Instead of creating one long bed at either side or back of the property, you could create a series of small beds with trees, large shrubs, or tall, ornamental grasses that would define the space. You could also plant containers, spaced evenly along the lot line. If the containers are particularly decorative, they could even be left unplanted. Another possibility is to use a series of benches, sculptures, or birdhouses to define the lines.

Second, learn which municipal zoning ordinances will impact the changes that you want to make. These ordinances usually determine how far from the lot line structures must be and what height fences can be without having to get permission from your neighbors and the zoning board.

IN THE FIRST YEAR

You will probably be eager to start making changes straight away, but it is actually very helpful to spend your first year—whether the first year in your home, or the first year after deciding to make a change—observing your landscape. Take extensive notes on how the hardscaping works for you, whether paths are lacking where you need them, which plants you have and how they change during the seasons, and also whether there are periods when nothing is happening in the landscape. Mulching will keep the weeds down while you wait, and the addition of compost or other organic material will improve the soil for when you're ready to begin planting. You can purchase some annuals for window boxes, hanging baskets, or containers that will provide instant color and satisfaction while you take the time to establish a reinvention plan.

Spend some time thinking about what kind of outdoor spaces you need for play, entertaining, dining, storage, specialty gardens, or other uses. This will help you to make decisions about where everything will be placed in your landscape and what size each space needs to be.

Think about your ideal landscape—your dream garden. Would it be formal or informal? These are the two basic styles of landscaping. Formal design is based on geometric patterns, most often using rectilinear forms, and was particularly common in France and Italy from the beginning of the Renaissance through the 20th century. Informal design is an attempt to create naturalistic use of space, often employing curvilinear forms.

Perhaps your dream landscape will be welcoming—without actually having a welcome mat—or you might want a traditional foundation planting, generally a row of evergreens in a narrow bed surrounding the house. Your landscape can be quiet and sterile or you could fill it with plants that attract birds, butterflies, and insects. Are there fragrant plants like heavily scented lilacs or roses in your landscape that remind you of your childhood?

◁ **These fragrant roses remind the homeowner of his mother's garden.**

▷ These rose garden arches are reminiscent of those seen in Monet's gardens in Giverny.

Determine whether you have outdoor spaces or rooms that feel like an extension of your home. If not, how can that be achieved? Your outdoor spaces should be just as much a reflection of who you are as the indoor spaces. Your outdoor space should be a refuge where you can relax, read, socialize, play, or listen to music.

It can even be a place for cooking. Do your dreams include an outdoor cooking area that is more than just a grill? What about an outdoor eating area? If there is an existing patio, perhaps it is close enough to the kitchen so that it would be convenient to bring out food and drink, plates, silver, and napkins; if not, you might want to add storage and serving space.

Consider the fond memories of places you visited when you were a child or where you grew up. If you spent time near the water, in the mountains, or in the woods, perhaps you can incorporate some elements of those locales into your landscape. These are happy memories, and it will be rewarding to be surrounded by them every day.

Also, think about locations that you have visited as an adult from which you can take inspiration for your new landscape. Many visitors to Monet's gardens in Giverny, France, upon their return home, have incorporated a series of arches similar to those they saw there.

Many people who visit English, French, and Italian gardens see very formal gardens that are exemplified by clipped hedges and specimen conifers. For those who fall in love with this type of landscaping, knot gardens could be created on a smaller scale. Keep in mind, however, that this type of garden requires a great deal of maintenance.

If you're inspired by Chinese or Japanese gardens, many of their elements can be incorporated into your landscape. Fence design has many possibilities as do the use

△ This very simple knot garden was created with two types of barberry (*Berberis* spp.) inside a ring of boxwood (*Buxus* spp.) at the Toledo Botanical Garden in Ohio.

of ornament and plant materials like bamboo. (Most bamboos, whether tall or short, spread extensively, so placement and maintenance are crucial. To avoid dealing with this problem, you can plant bamboo in a container or in a space from which it cannot escape.) Great attention is also paid to the design of stone walks, the patterns of which can be quite beautiful. Water and bridges are often incorporated in these gardens.

If you have children, there are many ways to create unique and natural outdoor play areas for them—and it will be so much easier to keep an eye on your kids if they're playing in your back yard. Get creative to provide places in the general landscape for kids to use their imagination, hide or shelter themselves, roll, jump, and run. And unlike play sets, these won't then have to be hauled away once your children are grown.

▽ The fence, roof, and lion statues at the entrance to this garden make it clear that you are entering a Japanese garden.

Finally, think about the specific types of gardens that you would like to have in your landscape. The possibilities are staggering: herb, vegetable, perennial, mixed border (amalgam of small trees, shrubs, perennials, ornamental grasses), wildflower, meadow or prairie, butterfly, bird, cutting, Chinese or Japanese, bog, children's, winter, and conifer gardens, to name only a few. Keep in mind that these types of gardens don't necessarily need to be separate but can be integrated into your landscape. Gauge your interest in sustainability, in permaculture. You can try things like diverting storm water runoff from your roof and drainpipes into rain barrels and cisterns instead of the sewer system so that it can be used for irrigation. Really, let your imagination run wild.

△ A gated tunnel dug into the underside of a grassy hill will provide hours of entertainment for children.

△ This swing, hung very low from a high tree branch, is intended for very young children, but can be raised as they age—and it will be easy to remove when no longer in use.

Establishing Your Budget

At this point, you know why you want to reinvent your landscape and have defined your goals. Before you go any further in the process, take time to analyze your financial situation. It is a giant waste of time to design the Taj Mahal if all you can afford is a log cabin.

Sometimes, though, you can afford more than you think—it comes down to your priorities. How badly do you want this? Of course most of us will not be able to get everything we want all at once, so make a list of the changes you have in mind and arrange them in order of importance. A design can be implemented in phases as you have the time and money to tackle each new project. Garden designs are typically implemented over a two- to five-year period, though you will probably make changes as you go along. Maintaining this attitude should help you to manage your financial anxiety. If at all possible, create a master plan, either by yourself or with the help of a landscape designer or landscape architect, so that when you put all the pieces together, you will have a unified design rather than pieces and parts.

When considering all that you want to achieve, be aware that those changes are not just a matter of plants and hardscape materials. You will probably need to amend the soil with organic and inorganic matter. This is not an inexpensive undertaking, as you will be paying for both the material and the labor to install it. Even if you elect to do the labor yourself, the soil amendments can still be expensive. Avoid sticker shock by being realistic; even for a relatively small bed, you can easily be looking at an investment of one to two thousand dollars.

Understanding Landscape Essentials

LANDSCAPES AND GARDENS CHANGE AS THEY MATURE, much like our lifestyles. To start reinventing your garden, take a hard, honest look at what you already have in place. Because changes in the garden often happen subtly over the years, it is easy to overlook them or become unaware of them. Even if you have been in your home for a while, and are looking for a change, pretend that you just bought the place and look at the landscape with as much objectivity as you can.

Depending on the size of your landscape and how elaborate you want to make it, you can redesign it yourself or look to professionals for help. Even if you call on a professional, however, be sure to have some ideas in mind for the way you want your landscape to ultimately look.

In evaluating your existing landscape, you may find that some plants don't perform as well as they used to. If they just need more or less light, transplant them to a more appropriate part of the garden and find new site-tolerant plants to replace them. Overgrown shrubs can often be trimmed back or removed entirely if no longer desirable. As much as it hurts emotionally and as much as it can be visually unattractive for a while, severe trimming (almost to the ground) can often rejuvenate old and woody shrubs. There are many books and websites that can walk you through the process of rejuvenation pruning.

A coordinated color scheme can really pull a landscape together and refresh one that may have gone stale. Think about the colors you have in your landscape now, and whether the combinations suit your taste. What colors do you have in your house? What colors do you wear? What colors make you feel good? Bringing the inside colors outside creates a sense of unity, thereby making the outdoors feel like an extension of your home.

The easiest part of renovating a landscape is deciding what to keep. In addition, keeping some older plants lends maturity to the landscape so that it doesn't scream "new." You already know which elements you like, so try to work with them. Deciding what to change is often more difficult because it entails defining exactly what in the landscape makes you unhappy. Don't feel as though you need to keep elements of the landscape just because they are there. View your landscape as if you are starting from scratch and only keep what really works for you.

Reinvention doesn't always have to be a major undertaking. Once you have a plan in place, small adjustments every year or two may keep you from having to start all over again. As the old adage goes, this is "addition by subtraction." Sometimes, just removing a plant or a feature you don't like is a vast improvement.

◁ This corner bed has one rhododendron that has been nibbled down to nothing and two scraggly deciduous shrubs which should either be pruned or taken out.

Environment

It is important to be aware that there are some environmental facets of your property that you will have to work with, whether you want to or not. While it is possible to change or tweak some of the conditions of your property, there is much that cannot be changed or can only be changed at great expense.

Before making any changes, assess these factors that will influence everything in your landscape. If you do not take the time to understand and consider them, you could be throwing your money away even if you have purchased the best plants or hardscaping available.

SOIL

Let's start with the nitty gritty—the soil. Many people take soil for granted, as do weeds, which will grow in virtually anything. Contrary to appearances, soil is very complex. Plants and soil life have a symbiotic (interdependent) relationship. Substances that plants exude from their roots attract and nourish beneficial soil life. In return, microbes in the soil, such as bacteria and fungi, create nutrients that plants need. The area in which plants and soil life exist is called the rhizosphere, which is often disturbed or destroyed by synthetic fertilizers, pesticides, and fungicides as well as frequent rototilling—one of the many reasons that I prefer not to use such materials and techniques.

This interdependent relationship between plants, microbes, and other soil life is known as the soil food web. This describes a series of conversions of energy and nutrients as one organism consumes another. All food webs are fueled by the primary producers: the plants, lichens, moss, photosynthetic bacteria, and algae that use the sun's energy to fix carbon dioxide from the atmosphere. Most other soil organisms get energy and carbon by consuming the organic compounds found in plants, other organisms, and waste by-products. A few bacteria get energy from other sources.

As organisms decompose complex materials, or consume other organisms, nutrients are converted from one form to another, and are made available to plants and to other soil organisms. All plants —grass, trees, shrubs, crops—depend on the soil food web for their nutrition.

Incorporation of organic matter into the soil provides raw material that bacteria and other soil organisms can convert into plant nutrients. Soil that is completely dry (or arid) cannot support beneficial bacteria, so some moisture is essential. On the other hand, soil that is too wet or too compacted lacks the oxygen that most plants need to survive. It also creates anaerobic (airless) conditions that result in a pretty unpleasant odor.

It is also important to know the pH level of your soil—whether it is acid, neutral, or alkaline. This often depends on where you live, but soil tests are easy and inexpensive. Many plants are very specific in their affinity for particular pH levels and planting them in the wrong soil guarantees death.

If you want to revise or improve your soil conditions, there are several ways to do so. Planting beds, as well as areas of turf, will benefit from soil amendment. There are a wide variety of materials with which you can amend soil, both organic and inorganic. The best organic materials are compost, leaf humus, and (well-aged) manures. These organic amendments can help sandy soils retain moisture and nutrients and help clay soils increase porosity and permeability while improving aeration. None of these materials are inexpensive.

In terms of inorganic amendments, I work mostly with clay soil and have learned to incorporate enlarged aggregate (shale, clay, or slate particles) in order to improve drainage. It is sold under a variety of brand names: Turface, Infield Soil Conditioner, and Haydite, among others. The aggregate is heated to very high temperatures and the resultant material is small, porous, lightweight particles that are capable of absorbing water and releasing it slowly at a later time while providing space for oxygen. It is much more effective than gypsum, which is frequently sold as a means of loosening clay soils. Because the particles are small, it is amazingly easy to dig in soil that has been amended with it.

Many gardeners make the mistake of thinking that sand would be useful in loosening clay soil, but the percentage needed would make its use exorbitantly expensive. Also, most sand particles are too small and would result in the creation of concrete, which is certainly not what we have in mind.

Vermiculite could be added to sandy soils to foster moisture retention.

Sheet Mulching

If you are blessed with patience, you can improve any kind of soil through a practice called sheet mulching. Sheet mulching is like making lasagna, but your ingredients are layers of compost, cardboard, and undecayed organic material. Before you begin, mow existing vegetation so that it lies flat. Remove only woody or bulky plant material. The remaining plants will decay and add nutrients to the soil. Soak the area with water to start the natural process of decomposition.

The first layer you will put down consists of enriched compost, poultry or stock manure, worm castings, or similar materials at a rate of about 50 pounds per 100 square feet. This will jump-start microbial activity. Then soak with water again.

The second layer is a permeable organic weed barrier that breaks down over time (in other words, do *not* use plastic). Cardboard, a thick layer of newspaper, or old natural-fiber carpets work well. Two or three layers may be required to achieve an adequate thickness. Be careful, though; if the weed barrier is applied too thickly, the soil can become anaerobic. Overlap pieces by 6–8 inches to completely cover the ground without any breaks; the elimination of light is crucial to prevent weed germination. This barrier prevents the germination and eventual emergence of weeds through your mulch. The weed barrier will disappear with time as it decomposes.

The third layer, about 3 inches deep, will be more compost, which must be weed-seed free. Well-conditioned compost, grass clippings, seaweed, and leaves are all ideal materials to spread over the weed barrier. If you are using grass clippings, however, be sure to mix them with another material; when laid too densely, they become anaerobic.

The fourth and final layer is a top dressing (mulch) that mimics the newly fallen organic matter of the forest (again, weed free). Good materials for this include leaves, twigs and small branches, fern or palm fronds (finely divided leaves), straw, coffee chaff (the remaining layer that remains on the green bean after processing but comes off during roasting; it can be obtained from coffee-roasting operations), wood chips, sawdust, bark, and so on. This top layer will slowly decompose into the lower layers, and, therefore, should be replaced periodically. This layer should be 3–5 inches deep.

If this is all done properly, there will never again be a need to turn the soil; earthworms will do the tilling for you. Your only remaining task will be to periodically replenish the mulch.

LIGHT

To maximize plant survival and growth and to decide where you want to place various hardscape features, it is crucial to evaluate how much light you have throughout your property. It is easy to look out your window in early spring and say that a particular area is sunny, but you may not have taken into account that the sunlight is only there because the nearby tree hasn't foliated yet. Likewise, a quick glance at your light levels in the morning does not mean that the amount of light will be the same in the afternoon.

For these reasons, I always encourage my clients to create sun and shade charts. You can divide your property into as many sections as you want and evaluate the light in each of them individually. The variations range from full sun to full morning sun or full afternoon sun, bright light, filtered light, or part shade, all the way to full shade where absolutely nothing will grow, not even a weed.

Ideally, you should create this chart in spring, in summer, and in fall because the angle of the sun differs with each season. (If you are too impatient, the most helpful chart is the summer one.) Only then are you really ready to select the appropriate plant material or hardscape site. Basically, it means waiting nine months to design and plant. Otherwise, it's a bit of a guessing game.

▷ A sun and shade chart allows you to plot the amount of light in given areas hour by hour on a given day.

BACKYARD

○ = FULL SUN ● = PART SHADE	A WEST BED	B NORTH BED, LEFT SIDE	C NORTH BED, RIGHT SIDE	D SOUTH BED
8:00 AM	○	○	●	●
9:00 AM	○	○	◐	●
10:00 AM	○	○	◐	●
11:00 AM	○	○	◐	●
12:00 PM	○	○	◐	◐
1:00 PM	◐	◐	◐	◐
2:00 PM	◐	◐	◐	◐
3:00 PM	◐	◐	◐	◐
4:00 PM	●	◐	○	○
5:00 PM	●	●	○	○

You can increase the amount of light on your property by removing trees (though I am always loath to recommend this because trees take so long to mature) or by having an arborist thin the branches of specific trees to allow more light beneath them. Conversely, you can increase the amount of shade by planting trees or tall hedges or by installing awnings or arbors, depending on the space that you want to shade.

If you notice that plants are leaning in a particular direction, it is likely that they are leaning toward the sun. Unless you want to spend time staking them, I suggest transplanting them to a sunnier space. If the leaves of some of your plants are scorching, this is an indication that they need a shadier spot.

Consider the light levels inside your house. Does the afternoon sun beat down on your house and make it feel too warm even if you have air conditioning? A large shade tree perfectly placed on the sunny side of the house might moderate that "sunstroke."

DRAINAGE

Investigate any unresolved drainage issues. Does rain water drain toward the house instead of away from it? Is there an area that is usually wet and, therefore, muddy and nearly impossible to mow? Do you want to prevent storm water runoff from going into the sewers or nearby bodies of water? These issues can often be resolved without a major investment in waterproofing or drainage systems. An area with poor drainage that has permanently moist (but not waterlogged) soil can be converted into a bog garden and

◁ A rain garden full of cardinal flower (*Lobelia cardinalis*) and ornamental grasses has been created on a sloped area between the house and the river in order to prevent storm water runoff.

thus a habitat for plants and creatures that thrive in such conditions. A rain garden is another option, though these need to be constructed so that they drain quickly.

If your house is relatively new, it is likely that your soil has been compacted by the machines used to dig your foundation. Since most plants need oxygen at their roots, loosening that soil is crucial to the survival of your future landscape.

Good drainage is essential. Sandy soils drain very well (perhaps too well), while clay soils drain poorly and slowly. More plants die from root rot (a condition frequently caused by overwatering) than from drought. Gardeners often cling to the "right plant, right place" mantra, which suggests that there is a skill to knowing where and what a plant's habitat (location in the wild) is; there are plants that are endemic to all types of soils: sandy, clay, wet, dry, acid, or alkaline. Understanding which type you have in your garden is crucial to selecting the right plants for your habitat. You can, sometimes, obviate the need to create good drainage through plant selection, but if the look you want is different than that created by the plants of a particular habitat, you will need to amend the soil to create that perfect environment.

Keep in mind that moss is an indication of wet spots on your property. If you encounter it, you can either raise the soil level, add drainage, or just enjoy it—some people would give anything to have moss growing in their gardens.

WIND

The way that wind affects your property may, in large part, depend on the area in which you live. Those subject to strong winds will probably want to plant tall evergreens as a windbreak in order to reduce winter heating bills. Over time, these trees are likely to lose some of their lower branches. Therefore, you may want to implement them with some lower evergreens or dense deciduous shrubs. This kind of living wall helps to dissipate the force of the wind and also protects other plants that have been sited within the boundaries of the "wall." Plantings of lower but dense evergreens in beds on the windy side of the house can act as insulation by creating dead airspace between the shrubs and the house.

MICROCLIMATES

Microclimates are present on any property. This means that although you live in a certain hardiness zone, there are spots on your property that are colder or warmer than your designated zone. You can find your hardiness zone by visiting the USDA's website (www.planthardiness.ars.usda.gov), though *Sunset* magazine offers their own zones that are even more specific (and particularly helpful to gardeners in the West and Southwest, as they account for several other factors besides low winter temperatures).

In the Northern Hemisphere, spaces on the north side of the house receive no full sun; thus the soil takes longer to warm and that warmth is a huge component of the beginnings of spring growth. Spaces on the south side of the house, unless shielded by

Protecting Against Fire

For those of you who live in areas that are drought prone and, therefore, combustible, precautions can be taken to help protect yourselves and your home against fire. Most of us outside the forestry or firefighter professions haven't given much thought to the fact that if a home fire or wildfire breaks out, some plant species are more flammable than others. If you live in such an environment, I suggest doing some research on these plants. I have seen many suggestions such as planting in small clusters rather than large masses, using low plants instead of tall ones near the house, and using decorative stone and gravel as mulch instead of most organic ones. I have included some publications on fire-wise landscaping in the book's resources section. Some cities, such as Rapid City, South Dakota, are even considering new legislation to prevent the spread of wildfires, laws that will specify which plants you may or may not use.

tall conifers, receive full sun all winter and warm the most quickly in spring. For example, in my garden I have a collection of hellebores. These evergreen perennials vary enormously in their time of bloom, depending on their location. The ones in the front of the house, facing south, usually bloom two months ahead of those at the back of the house, facing north, where they are additionally shaded by large evergreen shrubs.

In addition, remember that cold air migrates to low spots. You might, therefore, want to choose hardier plants for lower spots and for shady areas. Conversely, you might be able to grow plants that are supposedly not hardy in your region by siting them in sunnier beds that have excellent drainage. You never know if you can stretch the parameters until you try. Any failures are just part of the learning process.

ANIMALS

No matter how much thought you put into your landscape design, how well you prepare the beds, and how great your plant selections are, the process could be an exercise in futility if your new landscape is destroyed by marauders. Become acquainted with the various pests and destroyers in your area by talking to other gardeners and consulting with your local garden centers and botanical gardens and arboreta.

Deer Other than complaints about weeds and being unable to grow anything in dry shade, my clients' greatest concern is usually deer. No one wants to spend a fortune on landscaping only to have it decimated by deer chomping. Over the years, I have compiled a list of plants that deer will supposedly avoid. However, there are two problems with this list. One is that the deer don't always seem to have read it and the other is that my list and yours may differ because deer diets vary regionally.

The only way to guarantee a deer-proof landscape is to install 8-foot fencing, a very expensive proposition. I once visited a garden that used rusted steel reinforcing wire and posts, but there are other possibilities that take advantage of the poor depth

▷ This 8-foot deer fence is both strong and attractive, made more so by the brightly painted wire sculpture.

▽ This double-sided decorative fence, with supports set at 45 degree angles, can deter deer because it will affect their depth perception and discourage them from jumping over it.

Deer-Resistant Bulbs

Most gardeners are greatly dismayed by the fact that deer eat tulips like candy. Fortunately, there are many other bulbs that deer tend to ignore. These following hardy bulbs do not appear on the deer tasting menu.

Allium species (ornamental onion)

Anemone blanda (Grecian windflower)

Camassia species (camas lily)

Colchicum autumnale (autumn crocus)

Cyclamen species (cyclamen)

Eranthis species (winter aconite)

Eremurus species (foxtail lily)

Fritillaria species (fritillary)

Galanthus species (snowdrop)

Hyacinthoides hispanica (wood hyacinth, Spanish bluebell)

Hyacinthus species (hyacinth)

Ipheion uniflorum (spring starflower)

Leucojum aestivum (summer snowflake)

Lycoris radiata (spider lily)

Lycoris squamigera (naked lady)

Muscari species (grape hyacinth)

Narcissus species and cultivars (daffodil)

Puschkinia scilloides (striped squill)

Scilla species (squill)

perception of deer. You can try erecting an electrified 4-foot fence at a 45 degree angle. Or build a double-angled decorative fence. A third possibility is two fences, only 3–4 feet high, with 3–5 feet of open ground between the two rows. Deer will not jump into areas where they cannot see a place to land.

There are numerous repellent sprays you can try, but they need to be resprayed at least monthly, if not after every rain. Home remedies abound, though each will work only for a short period of time because deer are very adaptable. Large, barking dogs who run loose on your property are one of the best deterrents, assuming that you are a dog person.

Beyond these tactics, there are certain types of plants deer tend to stay away from or merely taste and say "Pfuh!": those that have herbal smells, are poisonous, are spiny (though this doesn't keep them from eating roses), have fuzzy or hairy leaves, or have fibrous foliage. In addition, if the plants are ferns, ornamental grasses, or members of the onion family, deer tend to ignore them.

Even though deer don't usually eat trees, they do rub against the bark so much that they can damage the tree irreparably. The best defense is a tree guard, a type of wrapping or fencing that goes around the base and trunk of the tree.

Deer are very much creatures of habit. Learn their routes. Amazingly, if a plant they love is not on the route, they might ignore it. Since deer tend to walk only where the footing is secure, you may be able to alter their route by staking pieces of chicken wire where you see scat or where you know their paths are.

Rabbits The villainous Mr. McGregor in *Peter Rabbit* found many nefarious ways to combat the hungry rabbits that entered his garden. While we must certainly approach them with more kindness than he did, they can be a burden for many gardeners. They are particularly fond of succulent vegetables as well as the young growth of many perennials. Holly Shimizu, now executive director of the US Botanic Garden, once said that she deterred rabbits by placing pruned rose canes at the base of plants that they might otherwise munch. They also are said to dislike onions and garlic, so try interplanting these with your favorite plants to discourage these cute but pesky animals. If you are growing vegetables, fence the beds with 3-foot-high chicken wire that goes another 4–6 inches below ground to prevent the rabbits from burrowing underneath.

Moles and voles Despite their similar appearance, moles and voles have different lines of attack for our gardens. Moles are carnivores that eat worms, grubs, and adult insects, whereas voles are vegetarians that gnaw on plant stems and grass. Voles will tunnel under your lawn, leaving it quite unsightly, while moles create volcano-like holes in the lawn by pushing mounds of dirt up to the surface, especially after extended periods of rain. Because their diets are different, so must be the baits that poison them. Squeamish as I am, I'd be calling in someone who specializes in pest control. If you'd prefer a more humane approach, you can purchase traps, but then you will have to deal with relocating any animals that you catch.

Raccoons and skunks Raccoons can damage lawns, especially recently sodded ones, by digging for earthworms and grubs. The Humane Society of the United States suggests the use of hot sauce (capsaicin) as a repellent on small areas. For larger areas, a band of repellent can be applied around the perimeter, motion-activated lights can be left on to confuse the raccoons or tip you off to their presence, and a scaring device, such as the ScareCrow sprinkler, can be set up to frighten any approaching raccoons. If raccoons are getting into your trash, a few commonsense steps will preclude further incursions. Try to keep your cans in the garage or a secure space until trash pickup day, purchase trash cans made to keep wildlife from getting inside, and secure the lids with bungee cords. The Humane Society's website has other suggestions that you might want to try.

Raccoons are not a large concern in my city garden, but I do deal with the occasional skunk. Skunks tend to build burrows under the house, so your best approach is to first have them trapped by a specialist. After that, I recommend creating a barrier that will prevent further burrow building.

Geese Geese are a problem wherever residential properties abut or are near water. Homeowners buy these properties because they love the sight of the water and opportunities for swimming, boating, or fishing, but they are often unaware of the goose problem until after they move in. Geese can be a nightmare for gardeners, mainly because of their prolific droppings. The Humane Society suggests the use of lasers and other light-emitting devices specially designed to scare birds at dusk, just as geese are settling down for the night. Scaring birds away from night roosts means they will start their day elsewhere. Unfortunately, these frequently advertised scare devices have little lasting effect.

Another option for discouraging geese is to use chemical repellents that make the grass less tasty. These chemicals can be either be dispersed as a fog or sprayed on grass to keep geese away from high-priority areas.

The most lasting way to avoid geese problems (and often the most cost-effective in the long run) is to change the habitat so that it no longer appeals to them. You can do this by taking away their preferred foods and creating a landscape where the birds don't feel safe—that is, by reducing lawn space, including dense, tall plantings along shorelines to make a barrier between the food and the water, and planting stands of trees between the water and grass so geese can't fly through.

Cats Neighboring cats often seem to see our flower beds as giant litter boxes, but there are many simple deterrents that you can try. Identify the areas cats seem to use the most and cover them with chicken wire. The holes in the wire will allow your plants to grow through but should discourage incursion by the cats. Choose wire with holes large enough so that their paws will not get stuck; the intent is to merely discourage walking there because the footing is uncomfortable. You can also try scattering natural objects, such as pinecones, the prickly fruit of sweet gum trees, or pruned thorny branches of barberry or roses on the ground in frequented areas. Be sure not to use anything that would cause physical harm to the cats. If it is your own cat using the garden rather than the litter box, try scooping up its feces and putting them in the litter box so that the cat can smell its own scent there.

Dogs The eternal battle between dogs and their gardening owners was usually won by the dogs until the invention of the invisible fence, an electronic pet containment system, which trains dogs to stay out of certain areas. Although these systems are quite effective, it is incumbent upon dog owners to also provide specific areas for shelter, exercise, digging, playing, drinking (providing plenty of fresh water in a bowl that can't be tipped over), and defecation. The simplest solution is to designate one or two places for defecation. It takes some work, but it is possible to train dogs to only use these areas. Choose a spot that is accessible and easy to clean, such as a gravel patch that you can hose down (I'm told that dogs often prefer gravel to grass). Alternatively, dog waste can be collected and flushed down the toilet where it will be treated by a sewage plant or septic system. You could also install some synthetic doggy turf that has drainage holes to prevent concentration and eliminate odors with a collection tray beneath. Several options are available.

Infrastructure

People often jump into landscaping projects without first taking a good look at their homes and the effect they have on their landscapes. Doing so can save a lot of money and many headaches. If you plan on doing any repairs to your house (or other existing structures), it is important to be patient and take care of those changes before embarking on any dramatic landscape overhauls. Among many other complications, workers will likely trample your beds, damage your shrubs, or throw their detritus into your garden beds during home repairs.

Things like installing retaining walls, lighting, extra electrical outlets, or gas lines are not always included when people first set out their goals. But if you have water or drainage problems, for instance, you will definitely want to make them part of your thinking. Not all of these changes will entail huge operations, but preparing ahead of time will save mess and money.

WATER

Most traditional houses will have been built with gutters and drainpipes that direct rain water into the sewer or septic system or into nearby rivers, streams, and lakes. As we learn more about water pollution and environmentally friendly practices that can reduce runoff, many of us are now attempting to keep that water on our properties so that it can filter down to replenish the water table or be reused to help cut down on water waste (and reduce the water bill).

Storm water runoff Water from rain and snow that hits your roof needs to flow into well-attached gutters that do not have holes or leaks. Otherwise, it will find its way down your walls and discolor or damage them. Check to see where your downspouts lead. Often this will be the sewer system, but sometimes they drain into your yard (and sometimes into your basement if not properly directed away from the house). If you prefer to use this water for irrigation, it can be diverted into rain barrels, an underground cistern, or beds that are far enough from the house so that water does not damage the foundation. While rain barrels are functional, they don't have to be ugly. They can even be painted in imaginative and fun colors and patterns to keep things interesting. If you have the space, you can also make use of this water by diverting it into a bioswale (a low-lying or depressed and often wet stretch of land) or a rain garden. Keep in mind however that as much thought should go into the planting design of a rain garden as into a perennial garden. Unfortunately, I have seen too many that are hastily planned and ugly, but they have the potential to be quite beautiful.

Irrigation Consider what will happen to your garden if you go on vacation or have to leave town periodically. Will your landscape survive if you don't ask or hire someone to water it for you? Do you need to update your existing irrigation system? If you don't have one, do you want to install one?

It is unfortunately not uncommon to see sprinkler systems running during a rain storm. Water is a precious resource (not to mention expensive), and this kind of waste should be highly discouraged. According to the best-management practices of the Irrigation Association and American Society of Irrigation, an irrigation system should have a rain sensor or a soil moisture sensor (or both) so that the system, which is usually on a timer, does not run while it is raining or if it has rained recently. At the very least, install moisture sensors that override timers in the event that you forget to turn them off. I would also encourage you to use subsurface or drip irrigation to lessen the

◁ Rain barrels painted in a dazzling array of patterns and scenes for a community project in Cleveland, Ohio.

▽ This beautiful rain garden is one of two that flank the entrance to the Saint Paul Hotel in Minnesota.

Bioswales and Rain Gardens

Bioswales are vegetated open trenches or channels that are designed specifically to temporarily store storm water until it infiltrates into the soil below while also returning water to the atmosphere through evapotranspiration. They should be planted with deep-rooted native grasses and forbs (perennials) that enhance infiltration, cooling, and cleansing of water in order to improve water quality before it reaches a river, pond, or stream. They can reduce runoff volumes and rates by slowing water down through the vegetation, thus allowing groundwater to recharge. Bioswales can be designed for wet or moist soil in sun or shade and plants must be selected accordingly. Poorly draining soils will need an underdrain system, basically perforated pipe that channels water to a filtering soil bed or outlet for overflow. If bioswales are to be accepted more widely, they need to be aesthetically pleasing; thus, maintenance is key. Invasive plants and those that are too aggressive must be regularly removed.

Rain gardens serve the same function as bioswales but are usually smaller and residential, although many are also found as street-side gardens in municipalities that are trying to keep storm water out of their sewer systems. These gardens are intended to divert storm water from the roof or lawn into temporary retention areas that are an aesthetic asset as well as a practical solution for that water. PVC pipe, laid underground, can move the water to the rain garden. The size of your rain garden will depend on the size and slope of the drainage area and the soil texture (I have included a link to a rain garden sizing worksheet in the resources section). Rain gardens usually have several levels; plants should be chosen depending on the depth at which they will be planted (before planting rain gardens generally look like a series of terraced hillsides). It is important to keep rain gardens far enough—at least 10 feet—from your home's foundation so that the water within the garden does not erode the structural beams of your home or seep into your basement.

amount of water that ends up as runoff or that evaporates into the air, which are both a giant waste of water and will raise your water bills.

Many irrigation systems, particularly for lawns, utilize rotors (spray heads), from which there can be a great deal of runoff. Although I strive to be water wise, my system is a combination of spray heads for lawn and drip for the beds. What you want to avoid is a too-wet, too-dry cycle that stresses the plants. (Note that in the process of installing many drip systems, I have learned that manufacturers of these systems often overestimate the width of the watering zone; the lines frequently need to be placed closer to each other than specified.) The efficacy of the system(s) you use will depend on your soil type, slope, root depth, plant material, microclimates, weather conditions, and water sources. I highly recommend hiring a certified or licensed and insured installer. Ask for recommendations from friends and neighbors who are satisfied with their irrigation specialists.

Try to group plants with similar water needs together. Doing so will create less stress on the plants, thus helping to keep them pest and disease free. Mulching will also help. Mulch that is composed of double-shredded hardwood bark or another organic material such as pine needles or pine fines retains moisture, smothers weeds, and adds nutrients to the soil. The material you use will be highly dependent on whatever is available in your region. Although shredded and dyed pallet mulches last longer and are cheaper, they do not absorb moisture as well nor do they decompose easily.

If you live in an apartment or a condominium, you are probably gardening in containers on your porch or a patio. What is your water source? Is there a spigot on the wall to which you can attach drip irrigation or do you have to fill your watering can in the kitchen? Watch the water as it leaks out of the containers and see where it goes. For individual containers, saucers will catch a lot of it, but for larger containers that are not movable, you will need a drainage system that ties into the balcony or rooftop drains.

RETAINING WALLS

Retaining walls are critically important in stabilizing hillsides and preventing soil erosion of raised beds where the soil might wash onto pathways or driveways. They can be constructed at any height. They also provide a solution for slopes that are difficult to mow. Even short residential slopes that are a continuation of the lawn need to be stabilized in some way. And if the wall and the plantings above it are attractive, the resale value of your home goes up.

▽ **This attractive retaining wall and its plantings, which took the place of a grassy slope, have the added benefit of increasing the resale value of the home.**

If you already have retaining walls, be sure to assess their condition and stability. When we moved into our home, there was an asphalt driveway that was bordered on the neighbor's side by their slightly sloped lawn and on our side by a one-foot-high retaining wall of rotting railroad timbers. We were pretty tapped out from our recent home purchase, so there was no money to replace the wall at that time and we lived with it for quite a while. Eventually the city housing inspector informed us that the asphalt driveway would have to be repaired. Fortunately, I had always hated that driveway. Since our house is a cream stucco, what I really wanted was a concrete driveway that would be tinted a pale beige. I also wanted to finally replace the railroad timbers—this was the perfect time to get that done. I chose a creamy beige barn stone (pieces of quarried stone that were formerly used as the foundation of a barn) as the replacement. What a difference those two elements make in the approach to the house.

If your retaining wall is made of dry laid stone, take a look at how it is holding up. Whether the stone is small or large (like barn stone), if the footings and backfill were not properly installed, gravity will eventually force the stone forward, creating gaps between the stones or between the stone and the earth; eventually the wall will fall. You may want to consider rebuilding it. If the wall is mortared, be sure to incorporate

△ For many years after moving in, the entrance to our house and gardens was an ugly asphalt driveway bordered by rotting railroad timbers.

△ The entrance to our home was greatly enhanced by the new concrete driveway and barn stone wall.

weep holes (small openings that allow water to drain from within) so that moisture can escape. Expert stone masons are rare. Anyone you hire should be bonded and offer examples of their work.

Retaining walls can also be built with pavers or interlocking concrete blocks. Paver walls can be very nice but the large interlocking concrete blocks are better suited to municipal or industrial sites (their only saving grace is that some of them have planting pockets so that much of the wall can be masked with greenery).

One of the problems with higher retaining walls is that they are usually quite stark. This starkness can be partially alleviated if the wall is terraced to accommodate a series of elevation changes and includes a planting bed or two, preferably filled with xeric (drought-tolerant) plants that will need little future attention unless the terraces are accessible.

Short retaining walls might also benefit from terracing, especially if built as a solution to a sunken area by the side or back of the house.

◁ **This eroding hillside has been faced with a series of attractive stone retaining walls, terraces, landings, and stairs.**

◁ **This relatively short retaining wall is built in two sections with a planting bed above the first section to diminish the impact of the wall outside the below-grade side door.**

ELECTRICAL WIRING AND OUTLETS

Think about the activities in which you might partake while enjoying your reinvented outdoor spaces. Maybe there are appliances you want to add—an outdoor heater, a stereo system, or a grill, for just a few examples. If any of these require electricity, you should take a look at the outlets that you have outside, and their positioning. Before adding any additional wiring and outlets, engage an electrician to evaluate your current system of fuse boxes, breakers, and existing lighting fixtures and timers. In most older homes, the systems are outdated and much of the wiring is not up to code. You can then discuss the options for adding new sources for outdoor appliances and accessories.

LIGHTING

Consider your lighting situation. Even if you don't plan to spend a lot of time outdoors in the evening, your view from inside would benefit from uplighting or downlighting trees and focal points. Uplighting house walls beautifies your home, but it has the added benefit of being a safety measure—fewer dark spaces for potential burglars.

Path lighting is also a safety measure for you and your guests, but you don't want to make the path look like an airport runway. Stagger light features on either side of the path to cast soft light instead of glare. You might also consider lighting any steps with one of the newer LEDs (light emitting diode) that can be attached to the lip of the tread or by inserting a light block into the riser. These lights use very little power.

LED or twinkle lights can be wound around tree limbs or arbors to attract attention to a beautiful shape or an entrance. Small perforated light fixtures (I call them fairy lights) that dangle from tree branches are fun, and they provide a subtle source of light.

Solar lighting is relatively inexpensive and usually pretty easy to install. Both low- and high-voltage lighting can be more complicated, so you may want to consider hiring a professional. If you do, I recommend hiring a lighting expert to do the work (and not your electrician)—artistry is key. Look at your friends' and neighbors' homes and ask for recommendations. If you get references from a lighting expert, try to visit them in the evening so you can see the work fully.

Whatever you do, remember that the key to effective lighting is subtlety, so don't go overboard.

◁ I have several fairy lights dangling from the tree branches near the path that provides access to my back yard. They have enhanced many an evening party.

△ Strands of LED lights illuminate this arbor and the path below.

▷ These granite steps are lit from the side for more subtle lighting.

△ **Instead of trying to hide the yellow hydrant behind her garden, this homeowner made it a part of the garden by planting perennials with yellow flowers and Bowles' golden sedge (*Carex elata* 'Aurea').**

△ **This otherwise ugly utility box near a stretch of museums and restaurants in Cleveland captures the image of a young woman enjoying some refreshment.**

PUBLIC UTILITIES

Some of us are unlucky enough to have utility boxes installed on our properties. Attempts by homeowners to disguise them with evergreens don't work very well because access to the box doors has to be maintained. None of us want to look at these ugly things. I can make only two suggestions. One is to install lattice panels that are as tall as the box and grow vines on them. The other is to hire an artist to paint a scene— flowers, or whatever pleases you—turning the box into a painter's canvas. But make sure you get approval from the utility company before doing anything to the box; I suspect there will be great variability in the responses, depending on where you live.

Fire hydrants are often eyesores, too. While painting these a different color is certainly not an option, you can try and make them part of your landscape. I once saw a brilliant solution in a Toronto suburb where the homeowner had planted bright yellow flowers and foliage into her beds to echo the color of the hydrant.

Maintenance

As we have already established, patience is a virtue throughout this process. Spend a year observing your landscape and note how much time you spend on maintenance. How often do you have to prune the shrubs? Why do you have to prune them and how long does this take? If you have perennials, how often do they have to be deadheaded for optimal appearance? How much time do you spend mowing the lawn? The answers to these questions should help you determine what to keep and what to change about your landscape.

◁ Left to grow naturally, these burning bushes would encroach on both driveways so the owners prune them into large meatballs instead of replacing them with more size-appropriate plants

◁ Snow-covered grasses, shrubs, and perennials look like sculptures while reminding us that the garden is merely sleeping.

Plant Selection

Pruning, deadheading, and weeding are not the totality of maintenance. There is also the matter of plant selection and spending time in the landscape and observing. For instance, ornamental trees, such as Japanese maples, and flowering trees have great impact without being high maintenance, whereas the maintenance of hedges can be a nightmare.

If you would prefer to hire a landscape contractor or professional gardener to take care of maintenance for you, be sure that the company does more than just mow lawns. Horticultural expertise is the name of the game here. A landscape designer with a maintenance crew, a professional gardener, or a company with horticultural maintenance personnel can immediately identify weed seedlings that need to be pulled or large "volunteers" (usually planted by the birds) that need to be dug out.

In addition, those who live in snowy climates should ponder where snow will be pushed by snow plows. It has to go somewhere and an area of brittle plants would not be optimal. Damaged plants will need extensive pruning in the spring. Such an area might best be planted with groundcover or perennials that die back to the ground during the winter.

Determining the level of maintenance with which you are comfortable is crucial. This is a factor that should be taken into consideration before renovation begins, as plant selection and placement will have great impact on the amount of upkeep involved with your garden. Most of my clients are pressed for time, so their main priorities are their careers and their families. While a low-maintenance landscape can certainly still be beautiful and interesting, it is critical that you make the right choices during the establishment of your garden.

A newly installed landscape rarely looks like the vision in your head. If you select plants that will not need much pruning when mature, they will probably look small and too far apart for the first three to five years. This bareness can be ameliorated with the addition of annuals during those early years. If you get anxious and use too many plants and put them too close together in order to simulate maturity, you are only creating future problems for yourself. You will either have to spend a lot of time pruning or you will need to move some of the plants to areas where they will have more space. Again, patience is key (I will emphasize this repeatedly).

APPEARANCE

Maintenance is also a matter of taste and personality. Many of our pruning practices are vestiges of the heritage that European gardeners brought with them when they migrated to the United States. They were used to formal landscapes with plants pruned into boxes and balls. Now, because this is what people are accustomed to seeing, this is

◁ This perennial and bulb garden looks somewhat sparse in its first June.

▷ Three years later, it is much fuller.

the way they think it should be. However, unless a very formal look is desired, necessitating a great deal of pruning, most shrubs look better in their natural form. I hate seeing otherwise beautiful plants turned into meatballs.

While precision is indeed desired by some gardeners, I prefer a more natural look in my garden. In fact, I strongly discourage the "fall cleanup," which is usually defined as cutting everything down and blowing all of the leaves out of the beds. Nature puts those leaves there for a reason; they are a natural mulch that decays and replenishes the soil with nutrients. The exception is raking or blowing leaves from groundcovers and lawn that will rot if the leaves remain. By leaving the perennials standing, we are providing food and shelter for birds, beneficial insects, and small animals as well as reminding ourselves that the landscape is merely dormant, not dead. In addition, if you live in an area with snowy winters, deadheads look like sculptures when covered with snow. Ornamental grasses are also glorious during the winter; it would be a shame to miss one of their greatest attributes.

WEEDS

Aside from deer, my clients are generally most irritated by weeds. How bad are yours? The answer to this question will vary depending on the area of the country in which you live, but identification is key to eradication. Your local garden center or extension agent will be able to help you identify the weeds in your garden so that you know how to deal with them.

Most weeds are easily controlled by simply pulling them, but some, like bindweed and thistle, can be a nightmare because their root systems are extensive and deep. In these cases, pulling is totally ineffective; you need to kill the roots. This, however, is easier said than done. Spraying with an herbicide over a long period of time works, but eternal vigilance is necessary. For bindweed and thistle, you should cut them back to a few inches and then spray every few days. New sprouts will arise nearby; watch for them so that you can spray immediately. This process will take at least a few years. Remember that glypsophate herbicides kill everything they touch, so use a cardboard shield to protect surrounding plants and only spray when there is no wind. If you do not want to use herbicides, you can try to douse them with white vinegar or boiling water, but these will merely burn the leaves; the roots will still survive. You can also continually cut these weeds to the ground and hope that the lack of chlorophyll will eventually cause their death.

If the weedy area does not contain any other plants that you want to save, or if any other plants present can be transplanted elsewhere (be sure to ensure that you are not also transplanting any weeds), you can try solarization. This is a process in which you totally cover the ground and let the sun kill everything under the cover. This process takes at least four to six weeks during the hottest months of the year, and longer in colder temperatures.

Follow these steps to solarize your soil:

1. Remove all plant matter.

2. Rototill the soil.

3. Level and smooth out the tilled area.

4. Water thoroughly.

5. Lay a clear tarp on the soil surface for at least four to eight weeks, depending on local conditions and the time of year.

Control of weeds before they germinate is also desirable. This is one of the functions that mulch performs. Pre-emergent herbicides, like Preen, are very effective. For an organic alternative, try corn gluten.

EVOLUTION

Regardless of whether you embark on this renovation project as a do-it-yourselfer or employ a landscape designer, keep in mind that landscapes are not static like paintings, but rather entities that evolve. Unlike an artist with a palette of paints, a gardener or designer is painting with living plants that change with the seasons and over time (the fourth dimension).

Over the years, trees get taller and cast deeper shade; volunteer trees appear and need to be removed; shrubs outgrow their original compactness. Tree growth probably affects lawns more than anything else (save for sidewalks, where the roots can cause upheaval), but all plants are affected. As a tree grows and matures, you may need to move plants that were once in sun but are now shaded by the tree canopy. Conversely, if a tree has to be removed, what once was shaded becomes sunny—and not all plants can adapt. Plants do not always follow their tags or gardening books, either. I have often transplanted a perennial or shrub because it grew larger than the space I had allocated for it.

Then, too, some things are not meant to be. I generally work with the three-strike rule: if I have tried a plant in three different locations and soil conditions, and the plant died all three times, then that plant is not going to work in my garden. If you are new to gardening, do not get discouraged by failures. Even the most experienced of gardeners have killed hundreds, if not thousands, of plants.

Evolution of Maintenance

As a plant fanatic, I avidly read plant catalogs and visit nurseries wherever I go. Although I have many "onesies" (the general rule of thumb is to always plant at least three of a kind), I have tried to integrate them into my gardens in a designed manner. In the last few years, I have finally accepted the fact that I am getting older and that I need to find ways of reducing the amount of maintenance required in my landscape. Thus, I deliberately try not to purchase perennials that need constant deadheading, shrubs that need to be cut back annually or deadheaded, and annuals that need to be planted every year (I realize that this is the definition of an annual, but I am relying more on those that reseed). Then I just have to edit (better known as pulling out and possibly transplanting, but mostly discarding) if there is too much of the same thing in one place.

HARDSCAPE

Hardscape features may also involve a degree of maintenance depending on the material and the feature. Even relatively simple water features, such as recirculating birdbaths, require maintenance at the beginning and end of the growing seasons if you live in a region that has freezing temperatures. Swimming pools evoke the tropics but they are expensive to install and maintain in any climate. Weeds show up between the paving of patios and sidewalks and need to be eliminated. There is almost nothing in your landscape that can be considered no-maintenance.

Themes

Take a good look at your house in comparison to your landscape. Are the two married? If not, changing or improving this relationship can result in a much more satisfying landscape. What is the architectural style of the house? Are its lines reflected in the landscape? If you have been lucky enough to purchase a historic home, but the landscape needs help, spend some time studying period-appropriate plants and hardscapes. Denise Adams and Laura Burchfield's *American Home Landscapes: A Design Guide to Creating Period Garden Styles* is an excellent resource.

If you are uncomfortable with your landscape's existing style or theme, you can partially allay that discomfort by replacing some of the shrubs or pruning them differently, as discussed in this book's opening chapter. However, if your discomfort is with the lines themselves, you may be presented with more costly alternatives.

Most landscapes are either formal or informal, and this is usually determined by the type of lines that define them. Architects and landscape designers call these lines "themes." Almost all homes can benefit from repetition of line, which is closely related to repetition of theme since theme is based on line. Look to architectural details for inspiration. Architectural lines could also be repeated in the design of swimming pools, especially when the pool is close to the house and both will be viewed at the same time.

If the bed lines you want to change abut any part of your lawn, it is merely a matter of digging to change the lines from rectilinear to curvilinear or vice-versa. To do this you will first need to determine the new depth (from front to back of bed). A flexible hose or rope is a very useful tool in determining new bed lines. Lay either on the ground to outline where you think the new bed lines should be and then adjust as needed. Use spray paint to mark the new lines, but only after you are certain that the lines will not be changed. To avoid spraying the hose or the rope, place flags along the rope or hose, remove the rope or hose, and then spray. If the bed lines you want to change abut paving, you may need to change the shape of the sidewalk.

Understanding and appreciating the different themes will help you determine which makes you feel comfortable and which best expresses the mood you wish to create in your landscape. It is also possible to mix themes, thereby creating unity of front and back spaces.

RECTILINEAR

A rectilinear theme is normally used to create a formal, symmetrical landscape. It employs a series of rectangles and squares connected by axes (lines crossing at 90 degree angles) that serve as paths from one area to another. The axes also divide the property into rooms. The quintessential, rectilinear, formal landscape can often be

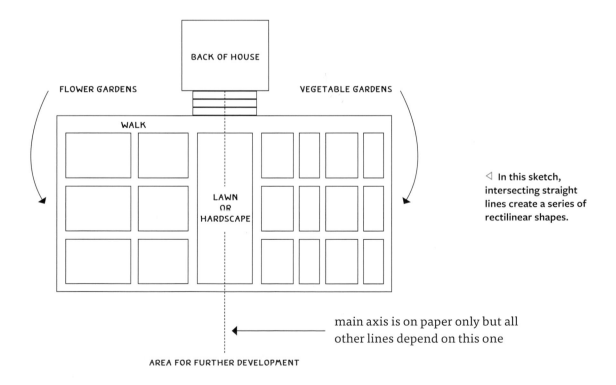

◁ In this sketch, intersecting straight lines create a series of rectilinear shapes.

main axis is on paper only but all other lines depend on this one

found in gardens in the southern United States that have beds edged with boxwood, in those of the Italian Renaissance that have long allées of Italian cypress, and in many English and French gardens.

This formality can, however, be countered with informal plantings within the hedged beds. A perfect example of this is the perennial and rose plantings at Sissinghurst Castle Garden in Kent, England, but I have even seen the essence of this combination of styles in a Dallas, Texas, landscape.

Most contemporary homes I've seen are very rectilinear. By adding long, linear steps to echo the lines of the house, the landscape and the house appear married to each other. If you erect a fence but construct it with horizontal panels instead of vertical ones, you can also echo the lines of the house.

A sense of interconnection is easily achieved with a rectilinear theme because one area will naturally lead to another. Think of rectilinear paths as a four-way intersection. You can either turn left or right or continue straight. As a motorist, you usually want to get from one place to another as quickly as possible. However, if you are walking through a landscape, the desire may be for you to take your time and enjoy the journey. If a path jogs, you will have to slow down.

With creativity, a rectilinear theme can be used to develop an asymmetrically balanced design. For instance, in a patio area, if a series of square pavers is used, leaving some empty spaces where pavers could have been, these spaces can be filled with small planting beds or interesting sculptures. Another long (the length of two or three

▷ **The English garden at Stan Hywet Hall and Gardens in Akron, Ohio, is a terrific example of symmetry. Almost every element on one side is mirrored in the other.**

△ The informality of Russian sage (*Perovskia atriplicifolia*) within these very formal hedges provides a refreshing contrast of styles.

◁ This terraced lawn has concrete steps with grass risers to echo the lines of the steps of a contemporary house and the pool.

pavers), low planting bed could be added to one side of the area, balanced by a vertical wall on the other side. Making use of both vertical and horizontal space allows for even greater creativity in your garden design.

Line theme can also be repeated in bed lines. Most houses have rectilinear doors and windows, but pitched (diagonal) roofs; combining both themes on the ground plane in walls, paths, and beds will produce a very unified design.

Architectural lines can be repeated with careful selection of plant material. The verticality of a narrow townhouse can be accentuated with pillars, but also with fastigiate (narrow and upright) trees such as English oak (*Quercus robur*). In another example, the lines of a long, low, shingle-covered house I visited in Long Island, New York, were accentuated by the horizontality of creeping juniper (*Juniperus horizontalis*) in front of it.

△ The design of this Kentucky home combines rectilinear, curvilinear, and diagonal lines. These lines are repeated in rectilinear beds with box-woods that have been pruned, some into mounded shapes and some into linear shapes.

◁ The landscape of this Frank Lloyd Wright home in Detroit, Michigan, is composed of a series of rectangles that zigzag for extra interest. A narrow gravel path leads from a clay tile patio close to the house to a large gravel patio used for larger parties.

△ The long horizontal roof line and the shingle pattern of the house are emphasized by the form of the junipers in front of it.

◁ The vertical lines of this narrow city home in Toronto are further emphasized by these fastigiate trees.

DIAGONAL

Rectangles, of course, can also be cut diagonally, thus creating triangles. A design conceived in diagonals can create extra interest on an otherwise boring piece of property. Frequently, this type of design is very formal, but I have also seen very interesting informal spaces created with diagonals.

One home I saw had distinctive diagonal paneling, and that line theme was repeated in the diagonal stairs that led to the front door. If the roof line or that of a portico is triangular, it could be doubled to become a diamond pattern in the path that leads to it.

▷ The designer of this brick sidewalk doubled the triangular porch roof line by flipping it down to create a diamond pattern in the walk.

△ The spaces left by this angled patio and the entrance walk have created diagonal planting beds. Additional points of interest are provided by the circular spaces inserted into the patio.

◁ The front of this house has unusual diagonal, wooden paneling. These lines are repeated in the design of the front staircase and the placement of the plants beside it.

△ The lines of these concrete containers echo the lines of the garage stone and door.

CURVILINEAR

A curvilinear theme tends to feel informal and relaxed. In order to give strength to the design, large, sweeping curves are highly preferable to a series of wormy squiggles. When designing curvilinear beds, it is best to try and avoid creating acute angled corners of lawn because they are very difficult to mow.

Try repeating the lines of a structure with ornament or in paving. The top of the door (decorative only) of my garage is curved and set into a stone arc, so I chose rounded concrete containers to place in front of it. A friend of mine used this idea on a much larger scale. A house with a porch was distinguished by an arched entrance that she echoed in the design of the adjoining patio and in the large step that accesses the patio from the back lawn. If your house has beautiful fanlights, you could use those lines as the basis for designing arced steps into the path from the public sidewalk or driveway to the front door when there is a grade change.

A series of island beds with echoing curvilinear lines is a visual asset. However, I often see one lonely island bed in a front lawn and wonder why it is there. Are there island beds that make sense? The decision of whether to keep the one bed or create more will likely depend on your time and how much of it you want to spend in the garden, but I strongly encourage you to give your beds some company.

◁ The large sweeping curves of this sandstone path and steps creates a sense of movement and ease.

▽ This new stone-edged patio echoes the stone below the windows of the house and its shape echoes that of the porch arch.

▷ Curved steps that echo the line of the fanlights above this house's windows provide a gracious entry.

▽ This series of curvilinear island beds, encircled with stone walls, breaks up a large expanse of lawn.

ARC AND TANGENT

This is a theme in which straight lines are connected to arcs, thus combining rectilinear and curvilinear themes. This, too, is a formal pattern but with a twist. An arc and tangent theme has a grace that the usual rectilinear theme lacks.

△ This arc and tangent courtyard serves as the entrance to a condominium. The fences that surround it are in a typical rectilinear design.

Working With Hardscape Elements

ALL LANDSCAPES ARE MADE UP OF THE PLANTS, SOIL amendments, and mulch—the softscape—about which most people think first, and everything else . The "everything else" could be walkways, patios, arbors, pergolas, walls, or even built-in fire pits. This is all known as hardscape. The hardscape is the foundation of your landscape; the plants are the decoration. When all the pieces of the hardscape are well designed, they tie everything together.

Evaluating Existing Hardscape

Sometimes the landscape we inherit is a hodgepodge. This often happens when there was no master plan, when previous garden projects were completed one at a time without giving any thought to how they might look in the future. As a result, the patio may be brick, the walks may be stone or concrete, the fence is either wood or metal, and the patterns are probably all different. To make matters worse, chances are that none of these materials relate to those with which the house was built.

While repetition of line is one way to marry the architecture of the house to the landscape, repetition of material is another method for creating this marriage. When evaluating your hardscape and considering changes, choose materials that can be added or substituted for some of the existing ones in order to develop unity out of disparity.

SIDEWALKS AND PATHS

When evaluating sidewalks, safety is the most important consideration. Is the walk uneven, or has part of it heaved? Look for spots where people are likely to trip and consider how (and how much it might cost) to have them repaired. Next consider the walk's design and how you might like to change or update it. Again, factor in the expense involved in making any changes. Once you have estimates, you can compare the relative costs of repairing the sidewalk or replacing it altogether.

When you take your first step on a path, do you think of the path as the quickest way to get from point A to point B or do you think of the path as a journey of discovery, adventure, and immersion in textures, colors, shapes, and fragrances that engage your senses? Perhaps the answer to this question turns on the design of the path as well as the material with which it is constructed.

The walkway that contractors frequently install from the driveway or the public sidewalk to the front door makes me cringe. This is typically a white concrete, narrow, and L-shaped path. This walk is merely a means to an end—arrival at a destination— and its placement so close to the house means that only one line of very small shrubs can be installed in beds next to the path. I prefer that guests feel welcomed. This can be accomplished through the design of the path and that of the beds next to the path. Instead of having your guests walk single file on a narrow walkway, why not have a path that is wide enough for two people to walk side by side? The width of the walk is also an accessibility issue. If you or your visitors need a wheelchair or perhaps crutches, your walk will need to be a minimum width of 3 feet, though 4–5 feet is preferable.

When considering the shape of your path, think beyond the typical straight lines that we see in most landscapes. Paths can be diagonal, which works particularly well when the architecture of the building emphasizes diagonals, either in the eaves of the house or the design of the windows or other integral structures. A path could also be a series of zigzags that enable those pushing baby strollers to stop and enjoy special collections or plantings specifically installed for interest and beauty. What's more, if the zigs and zags are large enough, the ultimate destination will not be immediately apparent and the walk will become a journey of discovery.

The same goal could be achieved with a long curving path, whether in one long curve or a series of curves, since it is difficult to see around a bend. Such a path would

▷ The sidewalk is so narrow that two people cannot walk side by side.

△ In order to direct focus to the homeowner's bonsai collection, this path was specifically designed with zigs and zags to slow the pace of the walker.

◁ The cut stone entry walk, set on the diagonal, echoes the roof lines of this traditional Cincinnati, Ohio, house.

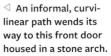

◁ An informal, curvi-linear path wends its way to this front door housed in a stone arch.

▷ The open gate of this fence and the wide path entrance convey a sense of welcome.

work best if the architecture of the house is partly curvilinear. Perhaps your windows are arched or the entrance porch is curved; this can easily be echoed in the design of your path. Path widths can also vary throughout the length of the walk. Establishing a wider entrance to the path can be particularly inviting.

As with most hardscape elements, there are a wide variety of pathway materials from which to choose. If the path is constructed of a material that echoes some facet of the building, it will have a positive effect on the way the path is first seen, even if only on a subconscious level. This might not seem like a complicated idea but its application is actually quite rare.

If the house has any brick in its facing, a brick or brick-colored paver path would add immeasurably to the charm of the scene. One of the attributes of brick is the number of patterns in which it can be laid. Running bond (brick laid end to end) flows from the beginning to the end of the path, making a short path seem longer. If this flow appeals to you, but the distance is considerable, the path can be broken up with ornamental diagonal or square patterns at sequential intervals. Another flowing pattern is herringbone. It, too, can be broken up with inserted circles, squares, or diamonds of brick or augmented with stone at either end.

▽ This homeowner went to the expense of converting the public sidewalk to brick so that it would blend with his home.

△ The curvilinear design of this running bond–patterned sidewalk makes it seem even longer than it would if the walk were a straight line.

▷ Large pieces of stone have been used to signal the beginning of a herringbone brick walk as well as the point at which it turns and continues on the perpendicular.

When laying a brick path, edging material should be used to keep the brick from moving out over time. This edging should not be visible from above. Brick set vertically can be used as an edger to facilitate soil retention in abutting beds.

Stone is the other material most often used for paths. Many homes are partially faced with stone, so an echo of that color and material will help marry the building to the landscape. Large slabs of sandstone were frequently used to provide access to homes that were built at the turn of the 20th century. Newer homes would benefit from the use of stone because it imparts a sense of age once the elements of nature darken it a bit. Any number of patterns can be used with stone. Rectangular pieces set perpendicularly to each other or rectangular and square pieces create very interesting patterns that lead the eye to the desired destination. In an informal setting, planting pockets could be left for low-growing perennials.

If you have a stone path that is divided by a small body of water, like a stream, consider bridging the water with large pieces of stone or boulders as stepping stones—rather than a wooden bridge—in order to create continuity. Placing pieces slightly apart will necessitate a slowing of pace, all the better to appreciate the watery surroundings. Bridging stones over a very narrow stream could also be set so that a trickle of water runs between them.

▽ In this welcoming entrance, yellow-flowered perennials, allowed to seed into the cracks of the stone sidewalk, echo the color of the chairs on the front porch.

◁ The combination of squares and rectangles in this stone path makes it appear to zigzag even though it is straight.

Since stone is widely available in many different colors and textures, you can let your imagination run wild. Consider devising your paths with a variety of interesting patterns.

Concrete, whether smooth or pebbled, is one of the least expensive materials for a sidewalk, but it can still be very striking. Concrete can also be used for stepping stones, in virtually any shape that is desired: squares, circles, ovals, or random shapes. If you are handy or have an artistic friend, design a unique shape that can be used as a template for path pieces. These can then be set in gravel, aggregate, or grass.

Gravel is frequently used for paths in Europe, but less so in the United States. While crunching on gravel gives us both auditory and tactile experiences, it is not a comfortable walking experience unless the gravel is well-tamped. An alternative is to use pieces of stone set into the gravel at easy walking intervals. Rounded river stone is an acceptable option if it is compacted upon installation and the layer of gravel is kept to approximately 4 inches. Mixing larger river gravel with smaller gravel works too (the smaller gravel seems to fill the voids of the larger) and it doesn't sink or spread as badly when walked upon. When budgets are tight and the frequency of use is infrequent, gravel is a fine choice.

▽ A stone path continues to the other side of a stream by virtue of large stepping stone rocks.

△ Japanese-style gardens are well known for having paths with one material but several forms and textures.

◁ This concrete aggregate path is first edged with smooth river stones and then with stone pavers for three different textures in the same space.

◁ These handmade leaf-pattern stepping stones were created by a San Francisco artist for her own garden.

When paths link outdoor rooms, you can ease the transition between the rooms by one of three methods: use one material in different patterns, vary the degree of formality, or use a succession of materials. One back yard I visited used brick around a gravel patio to create two paths with different patterns that lead to separate destinations, an excellent example of the first method.

In Virginia, a homeowner used formal cut stone, interrupted with a few rectangular spaces filled with river stones, against the house as a terrace and path. This area was then succeeded by a river stone path that was edged with cut stone pieces as you moved away from the house.

All the options discussed here are applicable to front, back, and side paths, keeping in mind that front walks are usually more formal than others (this, however, is not a hard and fast rule, and largely depends on the architecture and setting of the house and the personality of the owners). There can be a lot more variability in back and side paths. Stone slabs or large rectangular pieces of concrete could be laid with narrow bands of grass, herbs (think low thymes), or gravel between. While large, cut stone pieces are often used, seemingly random stone in a broken glass pattern would be very appropriate in a country setting.

△ Next to the house, cut stone has been used to create a formal terrace, but there are also occasional spaces filled with river stone.

▷ The path from the terrace toward the gardens is composed of river stones that are occasionally edged with small rectangular pieces of stone that repeat the shape and color of the terrace stone.

△ A wide brick walk constructed in a basket weave pattern leads one way while a narrower, running bond–patterned walk leads elsewhere.

Of course, softscape is also an option for many paths. Grass is the first material that comes to mind, but it should be used for this purpose only in a full sun location. Grass in shade is difficult to maintain under any circumstances and this difficulty would be intensified by foot traffic. Mown grass paths are often found in meadows and orchards, but they could also be used between several beds. Some groundcovers, such as rupturewort (*Herniaria glabra*), creeping cinquefoil (*Potentilla neumanniana* 'Nana'), and elfin thyme (*Thymus serpyllum*), can also make good paths. Where foot traffic will be very heavy, stepping stones can be set into grass or groundcover, though keep in mind that a certain degree of maintenance will be required to keep the herbaceous material from engulfing the stone.

While many paths are laid on flat ground, those laid on a slope offer many possibilities. I visited a garden in Utah where large slabs of stone were used, laying another slab on top of the first to create a riser when the grade needed it. The undulation of this path reinforced the lay of the land. If, however, a path with no steps is needed, choose a design that leads the eye upward. In this instance, an arched or zigzag pattern works very well.

△ In this back yard, large stone slabs have been set into the grass, providing an opportunity to move from the formal area near the house to a gravel path that meanders through the woods.

▷ A rustic path of broken stone evokes a sense of place in a rural neighborhood in Sacramento, California.

△ A wide ribbon of lawn makes it easy to navigate along the extensive beds of this property.

◁ The designer of this landscape was a master at manipulating the earth and huge stone slabs. He created a path, with only a few steps, that gives the illusion of stone in its natural state.

Once a material and pattern have been chosen for your pathway, the last design step is deciding whether to add a decorative edge. This can be made with the same material that you used for the path itself but in a different pattern, or it could be a contrasting but compatible material. You could also look into adding gates, pillars, or an arbor to focus the eye on the house instead of the walk itself. Think about inserting patterns into an otherwise boring, gravel path with stones or other materials. Hard edges of a path can be softened by planting close to the path edge and allowing the plants to sprawl over onto the walkway. Bottom line: paths need not be boring. Try to make what's underfoot pleasurable rather than just utilitarian.

▷ This sweeping path that traverses a slope was designed with alternating arching patterns that direct the gaze upward.

▽ The decorative brick edge to this concrete walk has the added virtue of widening it, thus ensuring a more comfortable stroll.

△ The wide leaves of these hostas have been deliberately allowed to flow over the edge of this stepped stone and gravel path.

▷ The homeowner created "flowers" out of pavers and metal rings, digging them into the gravel path.

△ A driveway of large concrete squares has been made permeable by filling the expansion joints with gravel at this Dallas home.

DRIVEWAYS

If your driveway is in good shape, consider yourself lucky. If it's not, how bad is it? Can you live with it for now or is repair imminent? New layers of asphalt can only be laid so many times before the driveway starts to get too high. At that point you face a dilemma: jackhammer it out and start from scratch or change to concrete or pavers.

Asphalt is generally cheaper in the short run but needs repair more often than other materials; it should last 10–15 years. Porous asphalt, also known as chip and seal aggregate, is a mix of asphalt and fines (very small stones); it looks either gray or russet, has a grainy appearance, and should last 15–20 years. Paver and concrete driveways, the most expensive options, should last 25–30 years. As in most things, the higher initial cost could save you money in the long run.

Permeability also needs to be taken into consideration. Permeable driveways soak up storm water runoff and, therefore, lower your sewer bills while also benefitting the environment (many sewer districts determine your bill based on the percentage of impervious pavement on your property). Some municipalities do not allow gravel driveways, but if they are acceptable in yours, they are extremely permeable (though you do need to have additional gravel added on a regular basis). Or try a combination: I saw an ingenious driveway in Dallas composed of large concrete squares interspersed with gravel strips.

What about color? If your driveway is asphalt, you're stuck with black. If, however, you have concrete and it is the standard bright white, an expert concrete installer could tint or stain your driveway to a different color. It would have to be periodically resealed in order to retain the color. Another possibility is taking out some of the concrete and inserting brick or paver patterns at regular intervals and at the edges to alleviate the unending sea of concrete.

You might consider a brick driveway or drive court (a combination of driveway and parking spaces), particularly if you own a brick house. Both brick and pavers allow you to choose from a wide variety of patterns. One of the factors to consider is the amount of time involved in laying the pattern and whether the pattern will necessitate cutting the material. Try to avoid patterns that would entail massive amounts of cutting; the labor involved will increase the price exponentially. However, combining two simple patterns, one vertical and one horizontal, will not.

Finally, consider the width of your driveway. I frequently see driveways where visitors get out of the car and then are immediately forced to walk on the grass—far from ideal. Regardless of the material with which the driveway was constructed, you can widen it by cutting out some of the lawn and replacing it with cut stone, brick, or pavers in a pleasing pattern.

△ This wide concrete driveway is edged with brick and some of the expansion joints are filled with brick to relieve the monotony of the vast expanse of white concrete.

△ This brick and stone paver drive court repeats the color and material of the house as well as the color and material of the steps.

△ For visual interest, this brick driveway was laid in a horizontal running bond pattern but edged in a vertical running bond pattern.

△ This driveway was widened with a strip of pavers that are similar in color to the drive and to the house.

PATIOS

If you already have a patio, it may be possible to improve it without major expense, assuming that it just needs tweaking. If the surface is even but ugly, it could be improved with cleaning or by laying a new surface, such as tinted or stamped concrete, over it. Conversely, if the patio paving is not in good condition or is poorly laid, you need to seriously consider replacing it, or at least re-laying it on a new, possibly permeable bed.

Before you proceed, ask yourself how large a patio you need. Who and how many people will be using it (think about how often you will entertain guests)? Consider how many dining tables and chairs you will need, and at what size(s). Keep in mind that you need to allow space for chairs to be pushed back from the table. How about other furniture, such as loungers, side tables, umbrellas, or planters?

Once you determine the size of the patio you want, think about its placement. Many patios have been constructed so that they abut the house, but there are two problems with this placement. The first and most dangerous is that storm water runoff may flow toward the house instead of away from it. The other problem is one of aesthetics. If you are sitting on your patio, it isn't exactly ideal to be looking at the wall of your house. Wouldn't you rather look at a lovely mix of shrubs, flowers, vegetables, and grasses that might attract birds and butterflies? Even a very narrow bed would be sufficient for vines that could be trained onto some type of trellis. Alternatively, you could plant vines in a series of containers, some of which might have tall obelisks, to provide support.

Look at the area where the existing patio is or where you think you want it to be. What kind of light does it receive: full sun or partial shade or both? Think about the types of activities you will use the patio for and whether the amount of light might need to be modified by screening. If you plan on using the patio at night, you will need to install lighting. Does the patio need to be close to the house or is there a different section of the yard that would be better?

Think about the configuration of the patio. There is no law that says patios must be rectangular. Patio design can be diagonal or curvilinear. It can also be a series of spaces, denoted by different paving or design details. I have seen an excellent example of this in the back yard of a frame house that had vertical brick insets. The formal patio next to the house was laid with cut stone that reflected the color of the siding. Proceeding further into the yard, there was a second, less formal area for sunbathing and general relaxation. That one was composed of brick that echoed the house insets. Using two different paving materials differentiated the spaces but related them to each other.

Before any construction, you should consider laying conduit (through which electrical cable can be pushed) under the patio to provide for future needs. Will you need water lines for an outdoor kitchen? What about gas lines? These lines should all be accounted for before installation. If you live in an area of alternate thawing and freezing, be sure that drainage of and the appropriate base for the patio are in place. Whether you do this work yourself, or find a contractor to do it for you, you will save yourself time and money by doing this work up front.

◁ The patio design theme here is arc and tangent, repeating the window lines of this Dallas home.

▽ The materials of the two patios adjacent to the house echo those used in construction of the house.

△ A narrow drainage area, filled with river stone, lies between the house and the patio. A clematis is being trained to grow on a section of steel reinforcing grid in order to make a large wall section more interesting.

△ This patio, shaded by an overhead arbor, has plenty of space for cooking and serving.

△ This pink tablecloth echoes the color of the roses on the wall but could easily be changed to lavender to echo the color of the petunias and ageratum.

△ A grouping of furniture on a small patio outside the front door of this house feels even more welcoming with the addition of a rug.

△ A tall trellis panel shields this sitting area from the neighbors to make outdoor moments more private and enjoyable.

Once you have an established patio that you're happy with, furniture selection will reflect your taste and greatly impact the mood you wish to create. There are a wide range of materials from which to choose: wicker, various woods, metal, and vinyl. If your climate demands furniture that is impervious to the weather (so it doesn't have to be moved into the garage or other storage space), consider concrete or metal. Both are available in a wide range of styles, from contemporary to antique.

Manufacture of outdoor furnishings and cushions have come a long way but they are not indestructible. Some TLC is called for. Vacuuming of wicker and sponging of cushions with a solution of mild detergent and water (plus rinsing) will keep the fabric clean. Wood should be scrubbed to keep it mildew free. Metal should be wiped down a few times a year and may need paint or varnish if the finish bubbles.

The simple act of setting a colorful cloth on a table can make a furniture grouping seem more inviting. The color of the cloth can be varied to echo the color of flowers in the nearby garden or to suit the season. Even if the patio is typically shaded, something brightly colored, like a table umbrella, would add immeasurably to the experience.

Another suggestion that might initially feel a bit weird is to try sprucing things up with an area rug or two. We love to use them in our homes, after all; why not use them outside? You can purchase rugs specifically made for the outdoors to cover unsightly areas of patios until funds are available for repair or replacement. Such rugs can also be used to delineate large patios into smaller parts.

If your patio is sited in a location that is visible to neighbors, think about installing trellis panels that would provide more privacy and still allow for air circulation.

DECKS

Aside from patios, decks are the most used outdoor living spaces. Decks are elevated floors and usually constructed of wood or a wood-like, recycled product. Be sure to do extensive research on the assets and liabilities of various products before embarking on a deck project. I would encourage you to pick a material that will blend with your house.

Hardwood decking can withstand harsh weather; choices vary between oak, teak, and various other tropical hardwoods such as ipe. However, the harvesting of these woods often results in deforestation. While teak can be purchased from plantations that are certified for reforesting, the data on ipe is uncertain.

Softwood decking, such as Atlantic white cedar, northern white cedar, redwood, and western red cedar, is a less expensive choice but not as long lasting as the hardwoods. Old growth redwood is both fire resistant and impenetrable to fungi and insects but most redwood populations have been either decimated or incorporated into parks and preserves where they can no longer be logged. However, there are some firms that specialize in cutting salvaged redwood. The cedars are naturally resistant to rot, mildew, overall deterioration, and insects and fade to a silvery gray. White cedar has traditionally been used in the Northeast while western red cedar has been traditionally used in the West and Northwest.

▷ This deck was likely constructed of red-wood for its longevity, but the color is jarring.

▽ With the artful use of potted palms and other plants, this deck becomes a great place to relax.

Composite decking is another option, and the materials have improved greatly over the last five years. A combination of recycled plastic and wood pulp, available in various colors and finishes, and intended to reduce the chance of rot, these materials are capable of withstanding the effects of difficult winters. However, this material is not indestructible. The surface of the boards can be scratched rather easily and cannot be resurfaced. There are also some decking products that have no wood in them at all. Also, the cost (twice as much as hardwood) is a definite factor.

Regardless of the material you choose, all decks require annual maintenance to retain their longevity and appearance. Mildew forms on decking surfaces of all types and should be removed from a deck soon after it appears. Good maintenance practices include providing for proper water drainage; keeping the surface free of dirt, leaves, and other debris; and moving planters, benches, and other deck accessories from time to time to permit the deck beneath them to dry thoroughly. There are a variety of protective finishes that should be applied annually to preserve the decking material. While traditional water-repelling clear finishes allow wood to gray from the sun, colored products block UV rays to better maintain the original color.

The color of all decking materials will gradually fade when given long-term exposure to the sun. There is some debate over whether the color fade of composite decking is irreversible. Deck owners may have to live with color differences that appear over time between sun-exposed and shaded areas of their original deck. Wood decks can be completely restored and refinished at any time, providing a decking surface that looks virtually new.

Ask friends and neighbors about their decks and any issues they've encountered. I also strongly recommend consulting a professional. A deck is generally not a do-it-yourself project. Make sure your contractor is experienced with the product you want to use.

If your property already has a deck in place, are you satisfied with it? All too frequently, a deck is merely a wooden floor that serves as an entertainment space. It can, however, be so much more. For instance, one Minnesota homeowner cut out an opening in his deck for a small pool. Another home I visited featured an enclosed deck with a fence painted the same gray color as the house so as not to detract from the surrounding woodland, along with built-in seating as well as a chiminea (free-standing fireplace) for cool evenings. A third homeowner spanned the space between the house and the swimming pool with a deck that became a separate room with planted containers deliberately placed beside and behind the chairs. Think about ways that you can enhance the visual impact and usability of your own deck.

FENCES

If you have any existing fences on your property, spend some time evaluating them. Are they in good shape? Are they functional but boring? Do you want to change them? There are many ways to do so; color, height, pattern, and material are all up for revision. Take a look at the zoning ordinances in your community about height and necessary distance from the lot line before you initiate any changes or install new fencing. I do recommend that you make the fence color compatible with that of the house. I hate to see, for instance, a white fence around a house with cream trim. Another pet peeve is a fence pattern at odds with a porch railing pattern.

And there are no fence police to say that fences can only be white, beige, gray, or black. If you love a particular color, be bold and use it to paint your fence. While touring in Germany, a bright yellow garden fence that I passed by really brightened my spirits. If your fence is on the property line, you can leave the neighbor's side unpainted while doing whatever your heart desires with your side. If painting the whole fence feels too bold, you could paint only the posts. That's what I did with mine. I inherited a stockade fence, and a few years after I changed the trim color on my house from brown to aqua, I painted the fence posts aqua and topped them with copper caps.

Changing fence height will be difficult and may require a zoning permit. If the fence is made of wood and has a flat top, it might be possible to add a decorative topper. Changing the pattern or material will be nearly impossible without removing the existing fence and installing a new one—but then the possibilities are infinite. Fences, like walls, can also have varying heights. Such fences would most easily be constructed with wooden panels.

If you're not concerned with screening out an unpleasant view, you could simply install a series of painted posts or poles without any overhead structure or a series of obelisks or pedestals. These can be as decorative as your personality allows.

▷ Repeating the color of my house trim, I spray painted every other post of my stockade fence and then added copper caps that echo the color of my copper pot.

◁ A horizontally designed yellow fence effectively divides a very formal space from the informal, floriferous one behind it.

▽ The panels of this fence appear to vary in height but in reality, they have been installed to simulate the sloping grade of the property.

▷ The height of these fence panels varies as does the construction, which utilizes both wood and corrugated metal.

▽ A series of painted poles creates a colorful fence around a small patio.

The Off-Season

The hardscape and other unchanging elements in your garden make up the "bones" of your landscape. These are often the key to a successful garden. The best and truest way to test your yard's bones is to observe the landscape in late fall or winter, once the leaves have dropped. It should appear unified while flowing easily from one area to another. Try photographing your landscape in black and white to avoid the distraction of color. Then look carefully at the photos. Are the lines of the landscape balanced? As you look from one area to another, do the weights of the plant material seem balanced? Too many evergreens, for instance, will appear heavy.

Evaluate the areas where you and your guests walk when approaching and entering the house. Pay attention to the walkway leading to the door and the surrounding area. Does it guide and welcome visitors? Is it well lit? Is it safe? All of this should be visualized twice: when the ground is bare and when the ground and all other elements may be covered with snow.

It is crucial that the winter landscape also be viewed from indoors, as that is where many of us will spend our winters. This scrutiny should be made with an eye to locating not only specimen botanical elements but also hardscaping elements such as walls, pergolas, arches, trellises, statuary, and paths.

▽ When all of these plants are dormant during winter, this colorful, metal art piece will still brighten spirits.

Establishing Outdoor Rooms

Now that your head is full of shapes, patterns, and materials, let's take a moment to relax and regroup. This would be a great time to step back and think a bit more about how our outdoor spaces can be broken down and divided.

Would you spend more time outdoors if you had outdoor rooms, instead of just outdoor spaces? An outdoor space is amorphous but an indoor room is defined. Are your spaces defined or enclosed in any way? Just as the inside of a house has floors, walls, and ceilings, so, too, do outdoor rooms. By understanding and using these elements in your new design, you can create rooms out of wide open or boring spaces. By enclosing your space, you will also create a sense of privacy and haven.

CEILINGS

The basic ceiling of an outdoor room is the sky, but it can be "lowered" or made to seem smaller with a tree canopy or a built structure. Natural ceilings can make a property more comfortable for those who live there, depending on the needs and locale: shade from hot summer sun, warmth by leaving the area open to the rays of winter sun, protection from precipitation, or screening from tree droppings (leaves or fruit) or dust. The choice of material for any of these functions is wide but basically aesthetic.

Tree canopies are an obvious choice, and they create beautiful ceilings. Depending on selection, they can vary with the seasons, either with changing foliage color or through their flowers and fruit. They also provide a natural transition from the ground to the sky. Several trees in an extensive lawn can act as a punctuated ceiling. Or a series of trees can be planted along a walkway, an effect known as an allée. It is amazing how much an allée can change the temperature of the air. I will never forget walking through a large public garden in Paris on a very hot summer day, feeling quite wilted, when I was quickly revived while wandering down a path under a plane tree allée. Obviously, public allées require a lot of space, but smaller ones can be created in private spaces.

Structural ceilings, on the other hand, can be penetrable or impenetrable. Function will be the determining factor. Think about how your space will be used: for sunbathing, reading, dining, or all of the above? Do you need protection from precipitation? What is the angle of the sun's rays during the hours in which the space will be utilized? With these answers you can decide whether a lattice-type roof or a solid roof structure would be most appropriate. Either type of structure would lend itself to the installation of lights. Downlighting could also be installed in trees, but if the trees are not yet mature, this will be difficult.

The most common choice for an outdoor ceiling is a structure over a patio, usually a pergola so that light and air are available. Pergola-type roofs are particularly amenable to coverage with vines that soften the hard lines of a structure, but the choice of vine should be made very carefully. Grape vines, while lovely and quick-covering, also litter the area beneath. (One possible solution to the littering problem is the use of a large piece of screening affixed to the topside of the pergola.) Wisteria also grows quickly

△ A large Chinese dogwood (*Cornus kousa*) provides a natural ceiling over the walkway that leads to a statue of St. Fiacre at an Ohio public garden.

◁ The entrance to this Dallas, Texas, home is lined with trees, thus creating a mini allée that shades the pathway.

▷ A number of plants, like this blue Atlas cedar, can be trained to grow over a wide arch.

◁ The bougainvillea on this armature, composed of vertical steel pipe plus attached arcing pieces at the top, has grown so much that the armature is barely visible.

but is slow to flower. Its other drawback is the strength of the branches, which can pull down almost any structure not built of steel. While many of us grew up with Asian wisteria, American wisteria (*Wisteria frutescens*) and Kentucky wisteria (*Wisteria macrostachya*) are better bets. They are just as floriferous but not as vigorous or invasive. But one of the best vines for a pergola is clematis, of which there are a seemingly endless number of choices. Although slow- growing initially, coverage tends to be quite good after three years. In the meantime, annual vines such as morning glory could be used as a supplement.

△ Sailcloth here serves a double purpose: creating a ceiling and shading this patio.

However, I like to look for unique ceiling alternatives, which is a lot more fun and a better expression of personality. I once saw four clumps of bamboo (*Fargesia scabrida*) planted on the corners of a square; the canes were pulled to the middle and tied to devise a living bower. This could also be done with other tall plants that have flexible stems or trunks, when young, such as Atlas cedar (*Cedrus atlantica* 'Glauca Pendula'). The Japanese train shrubs and trees to grow in a particular direction by tying heavy stones to the tips of branches.

Another fascinating ceiling I saw was composed of two metal arches. Instead of being the same height, one was taller than the other and was placed on the perpendicular so that the four legs of the two arches made a circle rather than a square. You could even combine the two concepts by taking metal poles with arches and training either hardy vines or small trees to grow up and out, thus creating implied ceilings, the height of which you can easily control.

There are also materials both old and new that are being used in novel ways to create outdoor ceilings. Sailcloth, treated canvas, or Sunbrella-type fabrics, with reinforced eyelets near the edges, can be mounted on poles or beams as either taut or curved ceilings over seating areas. In regions with harsh winters, this material should be taken down before winter so that the weight of the snow doesn't pull it down. Painted screening with a finished edge could also be used as a ceiling (I recommend spraying it with marine paint so that the color is long-lasting).

CONSTRUCTED WALLS

Indoor walls create rooms within a building. Outdoor walls define spaces within a landscape, thus creating outdoor rooms. Unlike most indoor walls, however, those outside do not need to be straight. Let your imagination run wild; the options are endless.

In crowded communities, front walls can be constructed just inside the public sidewalk. These walls need be only 3 feet high to imply that visitors are welcome (you can see in) but intruders are not.

Walls can also be a series of curves. At Monticello, Thomas Jefferson created a sinuous brick boundary wall at the University of Virginia that is absolutely gorgeous. Even though it's built with only one layer of brick, its strength is derived from the curvilinear structure. Most of the wall has plantings on both sides of it. It is both utilitarian and beautiful. That idea has been used elsewhere at many different heights and with a variety of materials.

If you want to pique someone's curiosity about the next room, build windows into the wall. I've seen this done with window frames without the glass, with clay tiles set on their sides in a window frame, and with large openings cut into cement walls.

It doesn't necessarily have to be a full wall, either. Sometimes it's just enough to erect something that divides your rooms. I saw a unique room divider in a San Francisco garden that was constructed of white cement and wine bottles. Some of the bottles were blue and their color was repeated in four of the glazed containers in front of it.

▽ The stucco walls of this corner property in Palo Alto, California, are much more interesting because they are not constructed in a strictly geometric pattern but have several jogs instead.

△ In this garden, a low, curving stone wall is used to create a raised perennial bed.

◁ This low serpetine paver wall divides the pool area from the patio.

▷ The cement wall enclosing this patio has windows that look out on an arbor, a fountain, and the surrounding countryside.

▽ This ingenious wall is high enough to divide the garden and patio area into a room separate from the driveway.

Low walls, just like low hedges, can also serve as room dividers. Low walls have the added benefit of being able to serve as seating, particularly when constructed at the edges of a porch or patio or around a fire pit. On the other hand, sometimes it can be more effective to construct a wall with varying heights. Longer walls, in particular, become far more interesting with the added variety.

In many instances, constructed walls of brick, stone, wood, concrete, or stucco hide buildings or objects that would detract from your enjoyment of a defined space. I visited one Kentucky garden that was meant to be viewed from the back porch. The homeowner bordered one side with a row of trees but could still see his wide driveway. As a remedy, he commissioned the building of a brick wall just behind that row of trees.

In a nearby Cleveland suburb, there is a fence that was constructed high enough to come up almost to the eaves of the building behind it. It features a gate that functions as an implied entrance to the building. In reality, that building was a neighbor's garage, and the gate created an illusion that the property was more extensive than it really was. Both of these structures were very creative solutions for disguising problematic sightlines.

When possible—with budget being the biggest potential hurdle—walls should be constructed of materials that take their cues from the architecture and materials of the house itself. If a client wants a front entry courtyard but still desires privacy, walls of stucco, stone, or brick could be constructed in such a way that sightlines from street

◁ Pieces of barn stone act as seating on this back door walk.

▷ Without this brick wall, the homeowner, sitting on his back porch, would be looking at his driveway.

▽ A very long stone wall attracts the eye with its different colors, textures, and heights.

△ This stucco home sits back from a main street but the walls in front offer additional screening from traffic and noise.

△ A Corten steel enclosure shields the homeowners on their patio from those using the common area.

△ This colorful fence has a large mirror plus a storage shed that is painted the same color as the fence.

△ A front door and windows made of mirrors join a picket fence and herb garden to make this faux house seem real even though it is all an attempt to break up the magnitude of a very long fence.

△ The owners of this sustainable home engaged a bentwood artist to create a unique gate.

△ This hop vine–covered arbor constructed of painted steel beams invites one to come in and explore further.

△ An elaborate latticed arbor with seating acts as a doorway to the next room as well as a resting place.

traffic will be obstructed but space will be created for a comfortable sitting area that is beautifully planted. Stucco is difficult to maintain in harsher climates, but textured concrete is an alternative. While the house and the outside of the wall could be painted a standard white or cream, the inside of the wall could be painted in a more imaginative color, depending on the space and your taste.

Fences, of course, can also be used to create walls. There are many variations of standard fencing, but if you want something entirely different, the only limiting factors are your imagination and your budget. Fences can be constructed out of uncommon materials or recycled materials. If you own a contemporary house, where a white picket or a split rail fence don't seem appropriate, you could try using a modern material in a pattern reminiscent of a picket fence, or perhaps Corten steel, which was developed to eliminate the need for painting and repainting. Another option would be to paint metal panels and link them together.

On larger properties, fences can sometimes seem endless. One way to break up the monotony, other than periodically changing the height or planting extensively, is adding another element. It could be a mirror and a storage shed that seem to be part of the fence, a window in the fence, or even a trompe l'oeil cabin.

If your fence doesn't have a gate, do you want to add one? If you have one already, perhaps you'd like to replace it with something more unique. This is a great opportunity to be creative. I've seen garden gates designed with a garden tool theme and gates for musicians designed with instruments or a clef. Bentwood gates can be really interesting, too, if you can connect with someone skilled in the craft.

Many front fences have an arbor as an alternative to a gate. A tall fence, with an arbor to indicate the entrance, can act as a frame and screen for an interior courtyard. This type of arrangement is especially apt for a narrow, city property where space is at a premium.

Arches and arbors can provide an inviting entrance to any walkway on a property— and are not always attached to fences. In fact, you can grow a vine or pendulous narrow tree like a weeping Atlas cedar on an arbor and virtually disguise it. Arbors can also be used to direct visitors or to define a smaller space within a larger one.

LIVING WALLS

All of the walls mentioned so far create a sense of division, but living walls, usually referred to as hedges, can do this too. The traditional hedge wall is a fairly boring straight line of evenly pruned plants, but we can do better. Hedges can be pruned so that a rounded shape periodically breaks up the monotony. Or they don't have to be pruned at all if a looser look is desired and if the plant is chosen for a particular mature size that will not outgrow the space. Beautyberry (*Callicarpa* spp.) would fit the bill here, a graceful shrub that grows 3–6 feet high and wide with long, arching branches and magenta berries.

Hedges can also be planted in curving lines or zigzags. Piet Oudolf, an innovative Dutch designer, pioneered a different kind of shaping in his early gardens where he sculpted his hedges by pruning their tops into large swooping curves.

Although an evergreen hedge is desirable where the view on the other side is unsightly, why not use a composition of varying forms, heights, and textures if you have the space? A line—not necessarily straight—of deciduous trees behind a lower hedge, either deciduous or coniferous, is much more interesting than just a row of evergreens. Dense deciduous shrubs such as viburnums, forsythias, and ninebark (*Physocarpus* spp.), just to mention a few, have a fairly fast growth rate and would be excellent screens. For hedges, plant them closer together than you would for ornamental purposes. (As a general rule, two-thirds of their typical width should work for spacing.)

▽ Some shrubs, like this beautyberry (*Callicarpa* spp.), only need to be pruned if they start to outgrow their space. This hedge was planted at Franklin Park Conservatory in Columbus, Ohio, to lessen the amount of maintenance.

◁ The graceful lines
of purple moor grass
(*Molinia arundinacea*
'Transparent') echo
the curvilinear lines of
the hedge around it.

▷ The hedges in this
Dallas garden have
been sculpted into sev-
eral different heights
and shapes.

△ A mixed border of deciduous trees, hypericums, *Viburnum plicatum* f. *tomentosum* 'Mariesii', *Berberis thunbergii*, and perennials forms a screen that is impenetrable to the eye.

In cases where you do want to see something on the other side, windows can be cut into tall hedges, just as they can be inserted into impermeable walls. Wherever I travel, I am intrigued by such windows and doors that enable the viewer to see the landscape beyond the room that has been created. Sometimes, this view borrows the scene beyond, implying that the land belongs to the property from which you are viewing it. Other times, the view entices you into a neighboring room.

A totally different kind of living wall can be made with a combination of posts and wires with vines or shrubs trained onto the wires to create a green wall. Many different types of material can be used: climbing roses, clematis, pyracantha, grapes (*Vitis* spp.), *Picea abies* 'Pendula', and wisteria, just to name a few.

As another option, an allée of trees is not often thought of as a wall, but I like to think of the trunks as a wall with spaces. For a short wall of trees, try some of the dwarf crabapples like the Round Table Series or dwarf magnolias (the Girl Series). For a low-limbed tree, try European hornbeam (*Carpinus betulus* 'Fastigiata'), tower poplar (*Populus* ×*canescens* 'Tower'), or columnar English oak (*Quercus robur* 'Fastigiata').

A very old form of living wall is typically composed of stones or pavers, constructed with planting pockets so that the wall looks at least partially green and allows water runoff to drain behind the wall.

△ Ownership of the meadow beyond is implied by a gate that is set into an opening in this border of deciduous shrubs.

△ Pyracantha is growing on a structure of wire mesh attached to poles that are set 8 feet apart.

△ A crape myrtle (*Lagerstroemia* spp.) allée is a common sight in the southern United States. It is ornamented in this picture with pumpkins for a festival at the Dallas Arboretum.

△ The addition of plants with different forms and textures to this stone wall adds greatly to its beauty.

LIVING FLOORS: LAWNS AND GROUNDCOVER

Floors can also be constructed with both hard materials and plants. The biggest difference between indoor and outdoor floors is that as one walks from room to room indoors, there is no defined path. Outdoors, one may cross a lawn at any point although most other connections are defined paths.

Lawn, of course, is the most universal outdoor floor. It is soft underfoot, thus easily walked upon, even when barefoot, in good weather. It does, however, have many drawbacks (more on this later). Fortunately, there are other groundcovers that can be used as floors, ranging from those that can bear only minimal traffic to those that can withstand the punishment of constant traffic. There are several brand names for these types of groundcovers: Stepables, Jeepers Creepers, and Treadwell Plants, to name a few. The plant tags in these collections state the endurance level and the necessary light level.

CONSTRUCTED FLOOR MATERIALS

Aside from grass, the most commonly used floor materials are stone, brick, pavers, concrete, and gravel. Each has its merits and demerits. Choose a material that marries well with the color or architecture of your house.

Stone, to me, is the most beautiful material to use, but also the most expensive. There are many different kinds of stone, but choose one that does not crumble easily as floors must endure constant wear. When possible, use local stone; its use will contribute greatly to a sense of place. This practice saves money on delivery charges and also, in terms of sustainability, saves on fuel costs. In the United States, gray sandstone is quarried in northeast Ohio; bluestone is quarried in Pennsylvania and New York; granite abounds in the fields of New England. Red sandstone covers the mountains of Utah but would look bizarre in most eastern US locations.

Bluestone is less porous than sandstone and is frequently an excellent alternative to sandstone if being used in shady locations. When shaded, sandstone tends to become covered with moss and lichen and thus becomes slippery unless periodically power washed. Bluestone looks particularly beautiful when the full range of colors is used, rather than just the blue-gray.

Cut stone, whether the pieces are all the same size or used as a series of squares and rectangles, will be formal in nature. Irregular, split stone set in a random pattern will seem more informal and is better suited to a suburban or country setting.

Brick (clay paver) is often used as a sidewalk or patio material because it evokes a charming, old-world look. Both brick and concrete pavers are durable, although clay pavers do not fade over time. However, concrete pavers are available in a wider range of colors and shapes. Cost-wise, they are comparable.

If you decide to use clay pavers, fill the joints with sand. Do not use poly sand unless you can be absolutely sure that every particle of the poly sand will be brushed away.

◁ On this property an informal stone patio has been constructed between a tall mixed border and the house.

▽ A bluestone walk and patio uses the entire range of available colors to add variety to the walking experience.

Otherwise, any grain that remains on the brick will become a white spot. If you decide to use concrete pavers, you may fill the joints with sand or poly sand. The poly sand makes a tighter bond so that weeds are less likely to appear; however, this also means that the floor will not be permeable. It is therefore critical that the designed floor is graded away from the building and toward a landscape bed. Annual maintenance, cleaning, and resealing will improve appearance and durability.

If you want a sustainable floor, investigate pavers that are designed for drainage. There are three types: permeable pavers allow drainage through the gaps between pavers; pervious pavers allow drainage through the pavers themselves; and porous pavers consist of a cellular grid often made of concrete or polyethylene that allows drainage through cells that are typically filled with soil and grass seed or gravel. Regardless of the type of paver you choose, I suggest checking with the manufacturer for their preferred depths of sublayers.

Concrete has an infinite number of possible colors and textures and can be poured in any size and configuration. It doesn't have to be smooth. You can vary the pattern within each piece of concrete by sweeping it, while still wet, with a broom. It can also be textured with tiny pebbles. If you want anything other than stark white concrete, you will likely want to hire an expert. If a concrete contractor tells you that tinting the concrete will lessen the strength of the concrete, call someone else (this is both incorrect and usually means that the contractor would just rather not go to the trouble of washing out the mixer).

Expansion joints look like straight lines cut into the concrete. Fresh concrete is a fluid mass but as the material hardens, there is a reduction in volume or shrinkage. The expansion joints are used to control random cracking. Fortunately, there is room for creativity in the design of these joints. They don't have to be horizontal lines; they could be alternating diagonals instead of squares or rectangles.

While smaller concrete projects can certainly be handled by yourself, I strongly recommend that you hire a contractor for any major projects. There are too many pitfalls that could make your concrete less durable and less attractive, including the way in which saw cuts are made (they should coincide with the pattern). Saw cuts are a way to generate expansion joints. They should be done at predetermined spacing to control cracking. It is really important to cut concrete after it has obtained enough strength to keep it from raveling, but before cracks could be initiated internally. If you want stamped concrete (patterned or textured to resemble brick, stone, or other similar floor materials), you will definitely want to call in an expert; ask to see examples of past work that are at least three to five years old. If the coloring is not applied correctly, it will fade. Stamped concrete needs to be sealed, but keep in mind that the sealant can make the surface slippery.

Concrete floors have a more finished and appealing look if they are edged with another material like brick or brick-like pavers. This material could be a contrasting color or a similar color but with a different pattern. Another possibility is a narrow bed of pebbles beside the concrete.

△ Both this patio and the bull nose steps have been created with stamped concrete.

△ The brick edge and dividers give this polished and stained concrete patio a very sophisticated look.

Gravel flooring is seen most frequently in English and Mediterranean-style landscapes. It will need to be replenished periodically. There are many types of gravel to choose from; use one with sharp edges so that the particles don't roll. Stay away from pea gravel, which is almost impossible to walk on. I find that gravel works better for pathways than it does for patios because it is difficult to move chairs on gravel.

Once you have chosen your material, establishing a strong foundation or base is crucial. Without it, your floor will shift, and fixing it can be very costly. The first step in creating the base is determining how deep it needs to be. This depth will depend on the climate in your region, so do some research before making any decisions. Next you will excavate to that depth and then move the dirt. (Perhaps you can use it to create raised beds somewhere else on the property.)

At this point, there are two options. The first is to lay weed barrier so that the base material does not work its way down into the soil below. Then put down limestone screening and compact it in at least two layers. On top of that lay an inch of sand and compact it—tamp it down very firmly. Most contractors use a heavy roller to do this. At last, you are ready to lay the floor. If you live in a climate where the soil freezes, you must have some type of retention product (edging), at the outer edge, to keep the floor from moving. The best edging has an L shape so that part of it is under your top layer of floor and comes up the side to keep it from moving. If you are working with split stone that can vary in depth, use a base of screening and sand. It will enable you to rock the stone to make it level.

The second alternative is to pour a 4-inch-deep concrete pad, making sure that the pitch is away from the house and that the finish is extremely smooth. Then lay your stone or pavers on top of the concrete. The edging stone or pavers could be glued to the concrete instead of using a retention product. (There are many videos online that can walk you through this process.)

Considering New Features

Since you are contemplating reinventing your landscape, what features would you like to add that would increase your enjoyment? What have you seen elsewhere that appealed to you? Were any of these features included when you set your goals? Did you budget for them? If the answer is no, spend some time rethinking your priorities and budget to be sure they fit with your financial circumstances.

FIRE PITS

A fire pit is one of the easier elements to add to your landscape, but it will offer years and years of outdoor enjoyment. That said, be sure to check your local ordinances before installing one. Many municipalities have regulations on how and when you can burn. There also may be regulations on where you can place your fire pit, so you will want to have that information in hand.

The range of fire pit choices is quite wide, as is the cost. Simple, portable, copper fire pits can be purchased from most home improvement stores, though the prices can vary. Inground fire pits are another option, and their costs will vary depending on the design, size, location, and fuel source (wood or gas are the obvious options). If you would like a gas-fueled fire pit, a gas line will need to be installed if it doesn't already exist.

In terms of where to site the fire pit, think about how often you will use it. The more convenient the placement of your pit, the better the chance that it will be used more frequently. On the other hand, if the pit will only be used for special occasions, perhaps there is a lovely, out-of-the-way spot on the property that would be ideal.

Once the pit is dug, it could be lined with concrete pavers while the top edge (cap) could be covered with a wide range of materials. If you site the fire pit in the lawn, stone could be placed on top as the cap to prevent singeing of the grass. The stone should be set at the same level as the lawn or slightly lower for ease of mowing.

Aboveground fire pits are very attractive, but also the most expensive option. Most of the ones that I've seen in my travels are circular and constructed of stone or brick. One was made with large arced pieces of sandstone set on top of huge sandstone blocks that act as tiered seating. Another was composed of layered medium-sized stone set in a broken-glass pattern. A third was built with stone in alternating layers that created a formal pattern and then was capped with bluestone to match the patio floor. Use your imagination: a fire pit could also be a square or rectangle. Think about how many people might be sitting around it, and build your design from there.

◁ Comfortable chairs surround a fire pit made with colorful ceramic tiles. The pit is set into a small gravel patio on a narrow lot.

▽ A sunken fire pit set into this back lawn is surrounded by low stone seating walls.

Fire Pit Upkeep

Maintenance of your fire pit is crucial for both your own safety and the longevity of the pit. Keeping your fire pit clean between uses will maintain its appearance and prevent potential fires from forming outside the fire pit. Use a broom (an angled one will work best) to sweep the inside of the fire pit area. Sweep in one direction to prevent ash from being moved but not picked up. Then scoop out all of the ash as well as any pieces of wood. Clear the area around the fire pit for a perimeter of at least 10 feet. This will ensure that a floating ember doesn't start a fire. Be sure to extinguish the fire completely; by doing so, you will significantly extend the life of the stone.

When not in use, cover your fire pit with a waterproof vinyl tarp. This will limit the amount of cleaning required.

△ Stone slabs have been set into this hillside to function as seating and as the base for a stone fire pit.

◁ Irregular pieces of stone have been used to create a fire pit on a stone patio surrounded on one side by large stone boulders for seating.

◁ The pattern of the wall surrounding this fire pit patio has been repeated with smaller pieces in the construction of the fire pit. More formal pieces of cut stone have been used as the cap, echoing the formality of the stone used to build the patio.

SHEDS

If your garage is so cluttered that you can barely park your car in it, it might be time for a change. How great would it be to be able to house your lawn mowers and tools, potting supplies, and more in an attractive shed? Or perhaps you already have a shed that you find either ugly or just ordinary. In either instance, you can convert something pedestrian into an attractive focal point.

Your shed can be large or small, depending on your available space and needs; it can be simple or fanciful. If the shed is constructed of wood, the wood, paint color, and design could match that of the house. A shingled house could have a small shingled, fanciful tool shed. A carpenter friend of mine loves to create fun sheds, one of which has trellises on both sides of the door and is painted yellow, but could be painted any color to match an existing house.

On a garden tour in St. Louis, Missouri, I visited a property where the homeowner painted her shed a color that echoes her kitchen, the room from which she views the shed. If you don't want to go to the trouble of cutting openings for windows in a shed, you can create the illusion of windows by inserting mirrors into old window frames and then nailing them on each side of the door. Then, to further the illusion, you can add window boxes underneath and fill them with flowers.

△ ▷ **The owners of this home have constructed a shed that echoes the architecture and colors of their house.**

◁ This tool shed looks like a small house and could easily be enhanced with flowering vines or climbing roses.

△ The red toolshed and chairs in this garden beautifully echo the vibrant red and green kitchen that looks out upon the shed.

△ With the addition of a decorative door, faux windows, and window boxes, this aluminum-sided shed in Ontario could easily be mistaken for a small guest house.

HOT TUBS

If you're interested in adding a hot tub to your property, there are many things to consider. The more convenient it is, the more you will make use of it, so it would be best installed close to the house. If you have a ranch house with the master bedroom on the first floor, a logical site would be right outside your bedroom—especially if you have sliding doors that allow easy access. And if you don't have such doors, perhaps you want to think about cutting through a wall to have them installed. This is an expensive undertaking, of course, so if it is not a viable option, there are other locations to consider. The two most common sites for hot tubs are patios and decks. The hot tub can be placed on the patio itself or it can be placed in a bed adjacent to the patio.

An obvious problem with hot tubs, however, is that they are not terribly attractive. Consider encasing yours in material similar to that of the patio so that it seems part of the patio rather than an intruder. You could also consider inground placement as an alternative to aboveground. Another alternative, if applicable, would be to place the hot tub under a deck, space that is often wasted.

I saw another brilliant solution to this problem in a New Jersey garden. Where the back yard slopes steeply, there is a wooden staircase that leads you from the gated entrance up to the two-level deck. In between the levels, encased below one of the landings, is the hot tub with a hinged lid that is part of the landing. This is a very clever solution to a lack of space and the desire to hide the hot tub from view when it is not in use.

Many tubs are tall enough that you might need a small ladder or set of steps for access. Privacy may also be an issue if your house is close enough to your neighbors. Try to determine whether or not neighbors could see you when you are using the tub. A homeowner in Portland, Oregon, solved both problems by building steps from the patio nearly up to the top of the hot tub and curtaining off the space. Steps that match the material of the patio create a very classy surrounding for a hot tub.

▷ **This color-compatible hot tub has been sited on the house's patio near the dining area and fire pit.**

◁ Here the tub is accessible from the back porch and shielded from the neighbors for most of the year by a large deciduous tree.

▷ The color of this stone patio is echoed in the stone used to encase the circular spa.

△ Just outside the house, formerly a barn, and adjacent to the patio, this hot tub is sunk into the ground and set in the middle of wide paver panels. The color of the cover echoes that of the pergola in the background and the house exterior.

△ What looks like a wide step is actually a landing with a disguised hot tub lid.

◁ The use of stone steps that match the patio stone, as well as the addition of plants and ornaments on the steps, make this hot tub as unobtrusive as possible.

SWIMMING POOLS

There is a great deal of information to consider when installing a swimming pool. Make sure you do your research and consult various resources before embarking on the installation of one. While they cannot be addressed in full here, they are definitely something that many will consider when reinventing their landscapes. Obviously there are a multitude of shapes, copings, and deck materials from which to choose. The pools can be just a hole in the ground or much, much larger. If you are going to invest (and pools are a sizable investment), do not skimp on the pool designer or contractor. Be sure that whoever you hire to complete the work is bonded, or at least has a background in design, engineering, and construction practices, as well as remodeling and renovation. Get referrals from a local pool service firm or from friends and neighbors who have used firms that were referred to them by word of mouth. Really good firms rarely advertise because they don't need to. If word of mouth is not an easy source, I would suggest viewing firm portfolios at a local home and garden show. You can interview several firms at once and will then be better able to make an informed decision. Inquire about their pool design and building education. How many courses have they taken? Do they attend annual conferences to stay abreast of the latest updates and techniques? Ask for references. Call those references and find out when the pools were installed and whether there have been any problems. I also recommend gathering at least two estimates for the same project. Keep in mind, of course, that cheaper is not always better.

Enhancing What You Have

It is quite likely that there is much about your landscape that you find satisfactory, but perhaps not as exciting as it could be—we do not always need to start from scratch. To get ideas and inspiration, start collecting pictures of gardens and landscape features that appeal to you from books, magazines, and online resources (Pinterest and Houzz are excellent for this). Visit the websites of landscape designers and view their portfolios. You will be sure to garner ideas from their various projects. Also take pictures around your neighborhood or city, or on your travels, when something catches your eye. Keep a project folder at home for these ideas and inspirations or create an idea board to which you can tack your pictures. All of this will help you stay inspired as you work on your own landscape.

ARTISTRY

Adding elements of artistry to your landscape is a quick and easy way to enhance your surroundings. A standard arbor or pergola in your back yard, for example, can be transformed with the simple addition of long ribbons, creating a tactile experience at either or both ends of the structure. For sitting areas, exchanging old, uncomfortable

◁ Long, streaming, waterproof ribbons add a burst of color to an otherwise drab pergola.

chairs for new ones that are beautifully designed and, perhaps, cushioned, would not only enhance the visual experience of the space, but also add comfort and a desire to lengthen the experience of sitting there and enjoying it. These are just two of many ways that artistry can greatly enhance your landscape.

Color, of course, is a huge component of artistry. How much color you introduce to your landscape and where you apply it will depend on your personality, taste, and comfort level. Fences, gates, and walls are often quite pedestrian, but for someone of

△ The curvilinear design of these chairs invites us to sit down and enjoy the space.

an artistic nature, the design possibilities are limitless. What color are the doors of your home? Or your gates? What about the color of the house trim? Remember that all of these are part of your landscape and that is what everyone will usually see first. I visited a property in California where the homeowner's favorite color was blue, so much so that the entrance gates, the screen door of the house, and a garden room door were all painted the same shade of blue. Those painted doors really left an impression on me as a visitor.

What about adding color to other elements of your house? I once encountered an absolutely striking chimney that was painted yellow on a weathered, gray shingle house on Long Island, New York. Or consider painting your steps and railings with colors that exemplify your personality. We rarely see brick houses that have pink railings and risers with forest green treads, but if those are colors you love, why not? Then paint the porch furniture the same color as the treads or risers and pick cushion fabric with similar colors. When choosing furniture, think about coordinating the color with window frames, house trim, or even the color of the house itself. Color echo is a very effective tool.

◁ The blue entrance gates of this California property are very welcoming.

▽ The blue of the entrance gates is repeated in the color of the screen door at this otherwise drab house.

△ This homeowner's love of pink and green is reflected in her choice of color for the railings and stair risers of her home (left). Don't forget to include the color of the roof or the eaves (right) in your overall color scheme. From a distance, these are all part of the whole.

▷ The yellow chimney and ladder are integrated into the landscape by using a yellow false cypress (*Chamaecyparis pisifera*) in the foreground as a color echo.

ILLUMINATION

Playing with your lighting is another easy way to enhance your landscape, and it can be particularly dramatic in the winter season. Darkness envelops us so early during winter that we often feel starved of light. A house and landscape that are well lit will therefore feel welcoming, warm, and safe. While generally regarded as a method of emphasizing focal points, lighting can also, when well placed, improve our ability to see a specimen plant or ornament from inside as well as outside.

Lighting is much more effective if it is subtle and if the source is unseen. While most lighting is for emphasis or safety, the use of fairy lights can create a totally different effect. I'll never forget my first winter visit to the Tavern on the Green in New York's Central Park. All of the deciduous trees were lit with strands of tiny clear lights wound through the branches. It was like being in a magical fantasyland. It is a concept worth copying. These strands of lights could also be wound up and through an arch or an arbor in a gesture of welcome.

The sun (when it does appear) offers us another aspect of lighting: shadows. Study the landscape during winter to see where and when shadows are or can be cast on the ground or on significant walls and then choose plant material that will create those shadows.

◁ Branches of a nearby tree cast a pattern of shadows in front of a small prairie garden.

SCAVENGING AND REPURPOSING

Be resourceful: it is amazing what you can do with more time than money. When I was making plans to eventually redo the landscape in the front of my first house, I became a scavenger. I kept my eyes open for construction sites with piles of discarded boulders and bricks. Today I would probably also collect pieces of broken concrete of manageable size. Whatever I found, I stockpiled. The bricks used in the winding paths of my first front yard were all collected, not purchased.

All of the original sidewalks in my municipality are made of sandstone. When homeowners are cited for broken pieces and have to replace them, the old pieces are placed on the treelawn before being trucked to the service center where they can be purchased for less than new stone. However, if the pieces don't weigh too much, I take them before the city trucks get there. When I replaced the concrete patio at my current house with sandstone, I purchased it for a very reasonable price at the municipal service center. While this material may not be one used in your city, keep an eye on treelawns as a source of recyclable materials.

Repurposing objects and materials accomplishes three things at once. It cuts down on expenses, keeps things out of our landfills, and allows us to feel a sense of pride for contributing to the betterment of the environment. If you keep your eyes and mind open, you will find ways to repurpose materials from both near and far.

When we finally decided to replace our youngest son's blue enamel bunk bed, I was determined to find a way to reuse at least part of it. Once it was disassembled, I realized that I could take three of the long, tubular bars that held the mattresses in place, stand them on end, and sink them into the edge of my wet bed at intervals, thus creating an implied wall. Since the top ends are open, I have inserted tiny terracotta pots that are filled with an impermeable material to prevent water from filling the tubes and rusting them from the inside.

Children's swing sets and climbing gyms often become a burden when our children outgrow them, as these large pieces fill spaces that could be used in other ways. Rather than spending the money to have them taken apart and hauled away, think of alternatives for repurposing them. If you don't need the space for other projects, you can create a garden bed around the swing set and use it as support for climbing vines or even tomatoes and other vegetables that need to be caged or staked.

As you drive around your neighborhood, be on the lookout for arborists who are taking down large old trees. These can be recycled in a number of creative ways. Ask the arborist if the company would deliver a trunk or pieces of a trunk to your house. They might charge you a small fee, or they might do it for free so they don't have to chip it. These can be used to build unique furniture and other structures for your garden.

Thrift stores and flea markets are also great sources of materials that can be repurposed. I find that this kind of shopping is fun if you want to create something unusual for your garden. All you need is imagination. It never occurred to me to collect old bowling balls or old dishes for reuse in the garden, but I have seen both put to creative

△ After his children left home, this homeowner created two beds at the bottom of the swing set poles that then allowed clematis to grow up and over them.

△ This shaded bed is enhanced with tall, royal blue poles—repurposed from an old bunk bed—that lead the eye from one end of the bed to the other.

◁ Tree trunks can be sawn into tables and chairs.

△ Spruce up the entrance to your vegetable garden by adding an arbor and then decorating it with plates. It will whet your appetite.

△ This artistic homeowner placed bowling balls into terracotta pots to edge her outdoor staircase.

▽ Large pieces of concrete have been reused here as paving with easy-care sedges planted in between to soften the hard look.

use in my travels. Local salvage yards are also great sources of discarded concrete that can be reused for steps and paving.

One easy way to repurpose old materials is to think creatively when it comes to containers. Old birdbaths are ideal candidates for planters on pedestals. Trailing plants will hide any defects. Even if you are planning to use succulents in the basin, be sure there is a drainage hole—if it doesn't exist, drill one. I have also seen defunct wheelbarrows used as containers. In one Kentucky garden center that I visited I saw one with the tires removed so that the body became a large container planted with herbs. You can even fill a baby carriage or stroller. If you can't find a friend or family member to pass these on to once your children outgrow them, consider a second, innovative life for them as plant containers.

◁ We don't usually think of a wheelbarrow body as a container, but why not?

▷ A wicker baby carriage becomes a container when painted an eye-catching lavender and then filled with ivy.

ILLUSION

Let's say you want a water feature in your garden but either can't afford one right now or don't wish to take on the work involved in maintaining one; you could instead consider making use of illusion. Take another trip to a thrift store or flea market, but this time look for old mirrors and blue, green, or clear-colored glass. A mirror set into the ground will simulate reflections as if it were a body of water, thus creating an illusion of water. You could even take the illusion a step further and edge the mirror with stone or brick or concrete, as you would a small decorative pool.

If you have a small patio and want to create the visual effect of running water, create an irregular path of large tiles that lead to the adjacent garden bed. Then use cut glass between some of the tiles. The glass squares should be set lower than the tiles (simulating a boardwalk feeling) and stones can be put on top of some of the glass or under others, just as stones in water would not all be at the same height.

Mirrors can also be used to make small spaces seem larger. When framed and hung on a blank wall or fence, they can create the illusion of being windows into another space. Reflections, especially of existing foliage, can appear to double the space. They reflect light while also creating depth.

Additionally, illusion can be used to redirect the eye from or disguise something unseemly that is difficult to conceal. Many of us are stuck with ugly telephone poles in our back yards. We are not allowed to grow vines on them because that would impede access for service. What we can do is plant a conifer or tree that will grow at least 10–12 feet high (or higher, as needed)—just be sure that its mature height will not be taller than the telephone lines. That 10- to 12-foot-area will become what most of us see when we look in that direction; rarely do we look higher than that. Choose a spot far enough from the pole to allow for the mature diameter of the plant.

Air conditioners, as we have seen already, are often eyesores on our properties. While we can surround them with an enclosure, sometimes it can be cheaper and perhaps prettier to surround them with a composition of plants tall and wide enough to hide the device.

Perhaps the roof line of your neighbor's house or garage impinges on your view of your own back yard. Pick your viewing spot and a site for an arbor. Then have someone else stand back with a very tall pole and a marker to see how high the horizontal line of an arbor would need to be to replicate and thus hide that roof line. Use that height to establish your new arbor and decorate it as you wish.

◁ Instead of using plants to cover this wall, mirrors have been placed to make the space feel larger.

▽ Mirrors can be laid below and in between large pieces of tile "decking" to simulate water.

▽ Evergreen plants such as hollies are an excellent choice for hiding ugly air conditioners.

△ This shallow stone arch is filled with a mirror to create the illusion of additional garden rooms.

▷ This arbor and swing disguise the roof line of the house on the other side of the property line.

ORNAMENT

The range of choices for garden art, as I am sure you have experienced, is quite wide: from antique to contemporary, serious to whimsical, functional to funky, the options are endless. Art and ornament add a human element to our landscapes and have the added benefit of usually being transportable. You can even purchase objects while out of town and then install them in your landscape, thus encapsulating memories of your travels.

Before making a purchase, however, try to visualize where you would want to place the object. Will it be in scale with the space? Is the color compatible? No matter how much you love the art or ornament that you have purchased for the garden, if it is not well placed, it will not be fully enjoyed. When well placed, however, the viewer will stop and notice everything: the setting, the art, the plants surrounding it, and the light. Dark ornament needs a light background and light or pastel art will benefit from a dark background. Do you want the art to be boldly or subtly displayed? Do you want to see it immediately or do you want to make it the reward at the end of a journey?

Almost any space (either side of the front door, the patio, or a deck, to name just a few) would be enhanced with the addition of beautiful containers filled with interesting plants. Scale (the relationship between elements in the landscape) is important here; you want to choose appropriately sized containers so that they are in scale with the space into which they are placed. What looks large inside a store will often look smaller outside. Furthermore, the larger the container, the less often it will need to be watered. If you want your containers to retain interest during the coldest months, fill them with prunings from conifers, broadleaf evergreens, and berried shrubs. Just be sure to do this before the soil freezes. The containers could also be filled initially with ornamental grasses or conifers of unusual forms for year-round interest.

◁ A metal sculpture of a woman that is both whimsical and contemporary.

If money is in short supply, temporary ornament may be a short-term solution. With a few more trips to flea markets or thrift stores, you might find a collection of objects that could be grouped in a large bowl or attached to a painted board. Why not buy several, colorful Christmas ornaments and hang them on the branches of your trees and larger shrubs? What about a collection of large toys? Door mirrors that are positioned to catch reflections and actually make the garden seem larger? In fall, you could purchase decorative pumpkins or gourds—I have only recently discovered the beautiful silver Jarrahdale pumpkin. All you need is a little bit of money and a lot of ingenuity.

◁ Eyes are drawn immediately to this metal horse sculpture, even from a distance.

▽ A silver pumpkin, set on Its side in a flower garden, is as ornamental as any more expensive sculpture.

◁ The jury is still out on whether or not this funky birdhouse will actually attract birds, but it definitely makes an impression.

FOCAL POINTS

Spend some time looking out your windows, walking out the front door, or following the walk to the driveway. Consider the different focal points in your landscape. Most properties have at least one. It could be a large shade tree, a weeping Japanese maple, a well-designed patio, a pergola, or an ornament such as a birdbath, sculpture, or large glazed pot. Think about whether or not you like the focal points and whether they are situated in the right places.

Many years ago, while visiting North Carolina for a conference, I fell in love with a birdbath that that I found at a nearby nursery. Fortunately, I had driven there and was able to purchase it and bring it home. I had a general idea of where I wanted to place the birdbath, so I put a stake in the ground at that spot and went inside and looked out at the location through one of my garden room windows. I was then able to go back outside and adjust the placement. It has been a great focal point in front of a fairly dull fence.

Walk down your pathways and consider the focal points that catch your eye. At my house, there is an arbored path that provides access to my back yard from the driveway. It actually took me quite some time to realize that there was no point on which to focus from the entrance of that path. The arbor acts as a frame, but there was merely an amorphous garden beyond until I added a Norway spruce (*Picea abies* 'Acrocona'), a slow-growing conifer with an irregular shape and purple cones, along with a large copper urn with an unusual swirled pattern. (As an added bonus, that urn, purchased in the Mexican town of Santa Clara del Cobre, where artisans only use copper, evokes memories of that trip.) For most situations, it is better to avoid having multiple focal points close together, but these two actually work because they are so different and play off one another.

Keep in mind that while weeping Japanese maples are frequently used as focal points because of their delicate foliage and undulating form, if they are planted too close to a sidewalk, they will encroach on the walking space. If that happens, and judicious pruning does not solve the problem, carefully transplant the maple farther back in that bed or to another bed.

◁ My birdbath is a focal point in front of an otherwise bland fence that will be covered later in the year with roses and clematis.

▷ While walking through the entrance arbor to my back yard, one's focus is drawn to the copper urn and the unusual conifer (*Picea abies* 'Acrocona').

BLANK WALLS

Perhaps you have some blank walls on your property or that face your property. Walls of homes, garages, and sheds are often not decorated in any fashion, but it can be fun to view them as blank canvases awaiting your unique touch. Imagination is your only limitation.

If your garage is as visual as the house, consider making the garage door an asset rather than a detriment. If you have the nerve (and the resources), you could even commission an artist to paint a scene on the door.

▷ While the brick wall shown here is not completely bare, it still could be enhanced with a climbing vine or some taller plants.

▷ The plaques on the wall of this St. Louis garage fill a large empty space that might otherwise be hidden by tall plants.

◁ This blank garage wall has become a focal point with the addition of a black metal sculpture.

▽ The heritage of this Native American homeowner in San Francisco is reflected in the painting on her garage door.

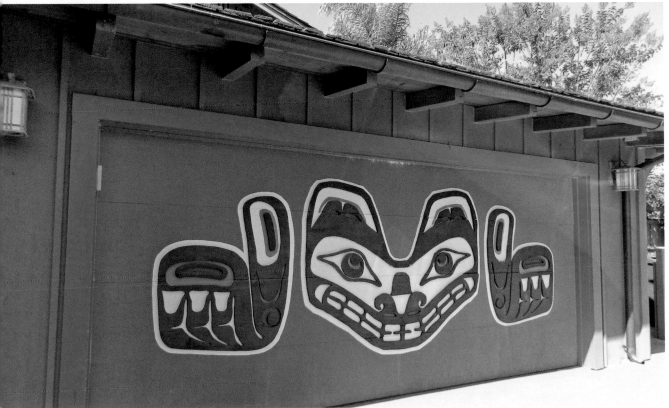

Assessing and Choosing New Plants

ONCE YOU HAVE TAKEN THE NECESSARY TIME to evaluate the other aspects of the landscape, it is finally time to turn to the plants. Despite the fact that there is an endless array of plant choices, the main reason that so many landscapes resemble one another is because they have been designed with a very limited plant palette. Diversity makes landscapes much more interesting, and it has the added bonus of preventing wholesale obliteration when pests arrive and decimate a particular genus. Different areas of the country have seen vast areas of tree death where pests with no natural predators have arrived. Diversity is also crucial for wildlife habitat.

The native habitat and cultural needs of plants vary enormously. What is perfect for a landscape in the Northwest will probably die in the Southeast. It's not enough to see a pretty picture; you need more information in order to create a beautiful landscape that will live and thrive.

In evaluating the plant material you already have, ask yourself if it looks healthy. Even if you don't know anything about plants, you can tell whether they are somewhat bare or full, whether they have broken branches, whether they have lots of dead-looking or browned-out sections, whether they lean when they should be straight, whether they are spindly, and whether they look like they were planted deliberately (some plants, known as volunteers, might have grown from seeds dropped by passing birds).

When selecting new plants, you will want to have a good sense of how much sunlight your property receives and what type of soil you have (this will affect its ability to retain moisture). Then you can think about whether you prefer deciduous or coniferous plants. Make sure that your plant selections take into account the mature size of the plant. Choosing plants that will outgrow their space means that you are needlessly adding increased maintenance to your busy schedule.

Trees

Trees, of course, are an essential component of any successful landscape. The word *tree* for me connotes a large, deciduous plant that will probably grow at least 10 feet tall, but more likely 20–30 feet or even taller. Evergreen trees, called conifers, also dot the landscape in comparable sizes. Sad to say, most of them are poorly sited in residential landscapes because the person who did the planting did not take into consideration their mature size.

Natives vs. Exotics

There is a great deal of debate at the moment about how important it is to use native plants. Some say that we should plant only natives in our landscapes because they are crucial to the survival of our native insects, especially caterpillars, and birds. Others say that a blend of both natives and exotics (species introduced either accidentally or deliberately by human actions into places beyond their natural geographic range) is more practical.

In fact, the definition of *native* itself is highly debatable. Native to where? Native to a particular state, region, or country? Is a plant native to North Carolina still considered a native if it is planted in Minnesota where it will live comfortably? As for exotics, we do know that some plants are deemed invasive. Generally speaking, this is because they have no natural predators and can grow at will, disrupting natural habitats. However, there are thousands of plants that grow elsewhere in habitats similar to ours and that do not have invasive tendencies (an invasive plant is one that takes over a space to such an extent that it displaces native plants). For instance, one of the most beloved ornamental trees in the United States is the crabapple, a native of Europe and Asia. Should this tree be removed from American landscapes simply because it is not a native?

So-called garden thugs are also a common concern. These are not necessarily considered invasive, but they are plants with extensive root systems that just keep spreading whether you want them to or not; they are very difficult to control.

I try not to be an ideologue about all of this; for me, the debate is not black or white. I look for new plants that have special attributes to fill specific needs in the landscape, and I do my research to ensure that I don't plant anything that would be considered invasive. Most states now have invasive plant lists (although some are better researched than others); you can avail yourself of this information in order to prevent further distribution of these particular plants. (*The Living Landscape*, by Rick Darke and Doug Tallamy, is the best exposition I've read on the importance and benefits of planting natives and how native plants can play essential as well as functional roles in gardens designed for multiple purposes.)

Look at your existing trees. Are they attractively branched? Many trees have dead or relatively bare lower limbs that detract from their appearance. You need to decide whether selective pruning will improve their appearance or whether your landscape would be better served by replacing them.

Even if you hate some of the trees in your landscape, you might be reluctant to remove them because they appear to be healthy and because it takes so long for them to mature. When we moved into our present house in 1983, the back yard had three hawthorns that were lovely in bloom and in fruit, but the stink nearly drove me crazy each spring. Still, although sorely tempted, I couldn't bear to take them out. In 1996, I was rescued by a late November snowstorm that blew in when all the leaves were still on the trees. By the end of the storm, two of the hawthorns had fallen out of the ground and one was irretrievably broken. What others would call disaster, I called opportunity.

Each was replaced with a special tree that I had seen in my travels but for which I formerly had no space. If any of your trees are leaning, diseased, or have dead branches, talk to an arborist for advice on which trees are worth saving and which should be removed. In some cases, trees may merely need to be pruned or fertilized.

SITING

We have already discussed the sense of claustrophobia that is created when trees are planted too close to the house, but another, more serious concern with this kind of placement is that a tree's branches will brush against the roof and the side of the house, potentially causing damage to the house itself. If sited too close to a sidewalk or driveway, trees might obscure sight lines and thus be hazardous. Also, avoid planting trees near sewer or water lines to prevent damage to those lines from the roots.

Of course, there are many problems that can be solved or alleviated through tree placement. If you live on a busy street with a lot of traffic noise, you can reduce it by up to 50 percent (according to the US Environmental Protection Agency) with some well-placed trees. It would also help if you raise the planting bed a bit and then beautify it by adding perennials and grasses on the street side and on the side facing your house.

Conifers can also be used as windbreaks and deciduous trees as sunscreens to moderate temperatures in the house and thus reduce your heating and cooling bills.

▽ **The trees at the back of this extensively planted berm act as noise filters.**

CHOOSING AND PLANTING NEW TREES

No matter how many great trees you currently have on your property, it's likely that you'll want to plant a new one at some point. As the old proverb goes, "The best time to plant a tree is twenty years ago. The second-best time is now." What's more, a new tree can even improve the air we breathe. In addition to cooling the air, tree foliage absorbs carbon dioxide and then releases oxygen in the process of photosynthesis; it also filters many impurities, such as dust, from the air. So get planting.

When choosing a new tree, think about its intended purpose. Will it be strictly ornamental for the patio or yard or for shade as well as flowering, fruiting, or fall color?

Most trees that flower do so in the spring: crabapples, ornamental cherries, ornamental pears, and magnolias, for example. There are a few that bloom in early or mid-summer such as sourwoods (*Oxydendrum arboreum*) and stewartias. If you want a tree that blooms in late summer, try seven-son flower (*Heptacodium miconioides*), a tough tree that thrives in almost any site that isn't overly wet.

Do your research ahead of time; don't just pick a tree because it looks good at the garden center. You need to know how tall and wide it will grow, what its cultural requirements are, what color its blossoms are if it blooms, whether it fruits and whether the fruits will present a maintenance problem, whether the bark exfoliates, and how fast it grows. In my front yard, I have an old crabapple, the branches of which overhang the sidewalk. Each autumn, I am continually sweeping up the fruits that litter the walk so that no one slips and falls—not exactly ideal. There are many region-specific reference books that can help you choose the best tree for your landscape (I have included several in the bibliography).

When selecting a tree for shade, keep in mind that its height should be in proportion to the size of the building and that it will need to be planted far enough from power lines to avoid any future mutilation from one of the power companies. If your house has solar panels, be sure that the new tree does not interfere with their collection of sunlight.

Before purchasing your tree of choice, examine the base of the tree. Can you see the root flare? Many nurseries unfortunately plant trees too deeply and the root flare is obscured. This means that the tree will likely be planted too deeply on your property when you get it home unless you remove the excess soil above the root flare so that you can see the proper depth for planting. Otherwise, the bark will remain moist and not be able to breathe. In addition, the excess soil may hide girdling roots, a condition in which the roots wind themselves around the lower trunk instead of spreading outward, thus ensuring the tree's slow death.

Landscape trees are usually sold as "B&B," meaning balled and burlapped. Large specimens can be expensive and very heavy, thus difficult to manipulate, but they do give the landscape a quick feeling of maturity. On the other hand, many studies show that smaller specimens adapt better and catch up in size within a few years.

◁ The brilliant fall
color of this maple
brightens the whole
landscape.

◁ The rosy sepals
of seven-son flower
(*Heptacodium miconi-
oides*) add another
month of color to the
fall landscape.

▷ This poor tree was planted under power lines and its mutilation by the power company was inevitable.

△ An example of how *not* to plant a tree: the root flare of this tree is buried so deeply that it cannot be seen.

△ This tree has been planted high enough that the root flare can be seen.

△ One of the easiest ways to keep a new tree alive is to use a treegator.

When it comes to planting the tree, theories have changed since I started gardening. The current philosophy emphasizes digging a hole at least as wide as the canopy and as deep as the root system. (I have included an excellent website with tree-planting directions in the resources.) Start by inserting a stake where you want the tree's trunk to be. Next, measure the diameter of the tree's root ball. Mark a circle around the stake, with either spray paint or cord, that's two to three times wider in diameter than the root ball.

Stand the tree upright and untie the burlap—without removing it—from around the base of the trunk. Carefully remove just enough soil from the top of the root ball to expose the root flare. If the tree is in a container, carefully find the root flare.

Measure the height of the root ball from the ground to the top of the exposed root flare. The hole you dig should be 2 inches less than the height of the root ball so that you don't bury the root flare. Use a pointed shovel to start your hole around the perimeter of the painted outline. If you need to remove grass, discard it or transplant it elsewhere but do not use it to backfill the hole.

Spread a plastic tarp beside the hole and shovel the soil onto the tarp so you can easily get it back into the hole when the time comes. Once the hole is dug, scrape the bottom of the hole flat.

Carefully carry or roll the tree into the hole. Stand back and view the tree as a helper slowly rotates it. Look for the tree's best face (every tree has one) and position it so the face is aimed in the most prominent direction—typically toward the street. Remove the wire basket from the root ball with bolt cutters or metal snips along with any twine or pins that are still holding the burlap. It is not necessary to remove the burlap from the very bottom of the root ball. It will rot away as long as it is not plasticized; if it is, however, all of it must be removed.

Mix some fertilizer in with the soil and then start to backfill. When the hole is full, tamp it down to create a shallow bowl so that water will not run off.

CARING FOR NEW TREES

My heart breaks every time I see a dead or dying young tree. This seems to be most common in tree lawns where a municipality planted new trees but the homeowner neglected to water them. Fortunately, some municipalities now install treegators when they plant new trees, and you can do the same for any trees that you plant yourself. Treegators are large plastic bags that slowly release water directly to the root system of the tree. Of course, the bag will need to be periodically refilled.

If you do not plan to use treegators, be sure to water approximately once every three days, preferably in the morning. Plan on giving the tree 5 gallons of water every three or four days. Do it slowly so that the water does not run off. This regimen can vary depending on daytime temperatures and rainfall, and your soil. If you don't water often enough, your tree will probably look like it is wilting. Keep watering for the first year. After it is established, a weekly watering will likely be enough, but as the tree grows, you will need to increase the amount of water. Plan to mulch with 2 inches of shredded hardwood bark to conserve moisture, but be sure to keep the mulch at least one inch away from the trunk.

While insufficient water is the number one tree killer, number two is damage from devices such as lawnmowers and weed whips that bump into the tree trunk and break up the bark. To prevent such damage, do not allow grass to grow up to the trunk. Dig a ring around the tree and mulch it. Unless damaged by storms, trees rarely need pruning in their early years. As they mature, and the ground below becomes shadier, you may want to consider having an arborist do some thinning of branches in order to let more light into the area beneath them.

Shrubs

Complaints about existing shrubs are some of the most common that I see during consultations with clients. They are frequently overgrown and hiding windows and doors. If your shrubs are taller than your windowsills, they are hiding the architecture of the house and keeping the interior in darkness. The first question to consider is whether or not they can be improved with pruning. Most deciduous shrubs take well to pruning

but coniferous ones are a different story. These will need to be pruned in stages and are likely to look terrible for at least a year (a resource on rejuvenation pruning has been included at the back of the book).

When analyzing the shrubs in your landscape, it is important to consider their seasonal interest. Many shrubs are interesting for only one season; you might, therefore, decide that these are not worthy of the space they take up on your property. Forsythia is an excellent example. Its bright yellow flowers are a harbinger of spring (if the flower buds don't freeze), but after that it is just a green shrub. On the other hand, many spireas are three-season wonders. For instance, *Spiraea japonica* 'Magic Carpet' has foliage that emerges as reddish orange in early spring and then changes to chartreuse for summer and fall. In late spring and summer, the shrub is covered with pink flowers. Then in the fall, the foliage turns rose and orange.

◁ These overgrown shrubs, blocking both the door and the front windows of this house, can be pruned, but it will likely be easier to just replace them with shrubs that will not require continual pruning.

△ The stunning new foliage of *Spiraea japonica* 'Magic Carpet' emerges in early spring.

△ However, during summer, the plant is notable for its pink flowers.

◁ When the temperatures drop in fall, the foliage takes center stage.

Even better, a mix of shrubs or a mixed border in which shrubs are integrated with perennials and grasses can further enliven a landscape and induce you to spend more time in it. If you are creating a mixed border, chose plants for their variety of forms, textures, leaf size and shape, heights, bloom time, and foliage color changes.

△ The use of color echo in this mixed border makes it very inviting.

EVERGREENS

There are two types of evergreen shrubs, broadleaf and coniferous. They retain their leaves or needles and typically remain green throughout the year, though there are exceptions. Some false cypress species (*Chamaecyparis* spp.), for example, change from green to purple or bronze or pink during the winter.

   Traditionally, evergreens are utilized by those who live in regions with colder winters so that some vestige of life can be maintained during the wintry months (though they certainly can have a place in any landscape, no matter the climate). However, their placement is crucial. In my travels through the cold and snowy Midwest, I never cease to be amazed and appalled by the siting of evergreens. In spite of the fact that most are intolerant of salt, they are frequently planted near the edges of properties where they are beset by salt spray from the street. To combat this, many people wrap their evergreens in burlap or install burlap fences that inevitably fall down before winter's end. But why have evergreens if you can't see them during the winter?

△ ▷ *Chamaecyparis thyoides* 'Red Star' is green during the growing season, but turns a pinkish purple in winter.

▷ These evergreens must wait until spring to throw off their chains of bondage.

Broadleaf evergreens, such as rhododendrons, azaleas, leucothoes, hollies (*Ilex* spp.), and Japanese pieris, are best placed on the shadier sides of the house so that they do not transpire heavily during the winter as they would if sited where the sun beats down on them. Most coniferous evergreens prefer full sun, but most false cypress, arborvitae, and hemlock species can tolerate partial shade, although they will probably not be as dense as they would be if placed in full sun.

HEDGES

Although a hedge is a common feature of existing landscapes, it is worth spending some time considering whether or not you want to keep the one you have. What shape is it in? Is it full of volunteer seedlings and vines? How much pruning will it need? What purpose does it serve? Does it screen out unsightly views or unwanted observation? Is it needed to define your property lines?

The three most commonly installed evergreen hedges in temperate climates are yew (*Taxus* spp.), false cypress (*Chamaecyparis* spp.), and juniper (*Juniperis* spp.). All have serious problems, however. The most serious is browning out, a common and unattractive occurrence whereby the green, flattened foliage turns brown. Pruning out browned foliage is rarely effective because those branches almost never refoliate.

◁ A well-sited, uniform arborvitae hedge creates a dense green wall.

American arborvitae (*Thuja occidentalis*) is another overused, tall evergreen that frequently does not fare well over time, particularly in regions with heavy snow, the weight of which causes the plant to splay (when an otherwise upright plant opens up, with branches spreading in different directions). I have found that the best arborvitae hedges are those planted in full sun on a north-south line.

Yew holds up very well, but is deer fodder if you live in an area that sees a lot of deer activity—and although hedges do need shaping, deer can be pretty erratic in the way they go about it. I often see eastern hemlock (*Tsuga canadensis*) used as a hedge in partially shaded areas but it tends to lose its density in those conditions. In full sun, it is lovely. In warmer climates, Italian cypress (*Cupressus sempervirens*) is often the plant of choice. In tight spaces, narrow evergreens or deciduous trees, such as English oak (*Quercus robur*), are obvious solutions.

Boxwood (*Buxus* spp.) is another commonly used evergreen hedge plant. It is attractive and works very well in formal gardens—and is avoided by deer—but when sheared too late (after the stems harden off in late spring), many stubs are left, marring the beauty of the plant. Hand pruning is the only solution, which can be time consuming and expensive. In addition, boxwoods are afflicted with several diseases and pests. Japanese holly (*Ilex crenata*) would be an excellent alternative if the desired hedge height is no higher than 4 feet. The shorter cultivars look quite good without any pruning. (Some tall cultivars do exist but they are difficult to find and they will splay from snow load if not tied.)

▷ The designer of this French-style garden used sheared boxwoods to outline each bed

▷ The informality of this *Ilex crenata* hedge lends itself to the soft curvilinear lines of the design.

The mistake I see most often with hedges, both evergreen and deciduous, is that allowance has not been made for mature growth. All too frequently, hedges overhang sidewalks and driveways. If they had been planted farther back, they would not be so troublesome. Forsythia is the poster child for this problem. When purchased, it appears very narrow, so it is often planted 2–3 feet from the driveway, where it will eventually become a problem. While this shrub does come back well after renewal pruning, it looks like it had a bad haircut when it is pruned back from the edges of driveways and sidewalks.

Several other deciduous shrubs commonly used as hedges are problematic. Foremost among them is privet (*Ligustrum* spp.), a shrub that I strongly encourage you to avoid. It seeds voluminously, is often infested with volunteer tree seedlings that are virtually impossible to eradicate unless caught when they are small (the roots are very strong), and becomes quite large unless pruned annually. How large? Alongside my fence on the south property line are two privet "trees." When we moved in 30 years ago, the privets were 15 feet high. Although I toyed with the idea of removing them, I left them in place because they blocked the view of the house next door. Wanting the height as well as more gardening space, I started by removing all branches below 8 feet. Ever since, I have had to prune out the new branches at the base at least twice a year. Privet is a classic example of a high-maintenance plant.

◁ When young and unpruned, golden privet (*Ligustrum* 'Vicaryi') can look quite good, but it will need extensive pruning and look very different as it grows taller and wider.

Burning bush (*Euonymus alatus*) is another problem child. In some states, it is considered an invasive plant because it seeds. It will easily grow 12–15 feet high and wide. The cultivar 'Compactus' is smaller, but will still be quite large, 8–10 feet high and wide. How often will you want to pull out the ladder to do your pruning? If the beautiful fall color of burning bush is what you seek, blueberry bushes (*Vaccinium* spp.) are a glorious alternative. There are multiple cultivars available with varying heights. On one visit to Oregon, a field of bright red blueberry bushes took my breath away. Even if the birds eat all the berries, you can still enjoy the fall foliage.

Two other commonly used hedge plants are barberry (*Berberis* spp.) and rose of Sharon (*Hibiscus syriacus*), though I discourage their use. Both are voluminous seeders, with only a few exceptions. The barberry exceptions are sterile or virtually sterile (cannot develop seeds) cultivars such as 'Concorde' and 'Golden Ruby', but they are too short to be used as hedges. Additionally, the thorns of barberry make pruning a fearsome task. Rose of Sharon, however, is one of my bugaboos. My neighbor planted it along our common property line and I am constantly pulling the seedlings, which have very strong roots. As if that's not bad enough, I also find the seedlings in my beds on the other side of the driveway. Although some sterile cultivars ('Aphrodite', 'Helene', 'Lucy', and 'Minerva') were developed in the 1960s, rumor has it that these may not be totally sterile). There is now a blue cultivar, Azurri Blue Satin, that is also touted as sterile, but it has not been in production and use very long. Always research which plants are deemed invasive in your location before planting anything new.

On the other hand, I can think of a number of shrubs that are not used enough as hedges. The leaves of hornbeam (*Carpinus* spp.) are green during spring and summer, turn golden yellow in fall, and are deep russet during winter, rather than bare as with most deciduous shrubs. This is a great asset if you have an ugly view that needs to be screened. Hornbeams can be sheared tightly or loosely, depending on the type of look you want. Happily, they also thrive in wet, clay soil, conditions in which many shrubs falter. The two most commonly used species are *C. betulus* (European hornbeam) and *C. caroliniana* (American hornbeam). European hornbeam, hardy only in zones 5–7, should be pruned during the first year to encourage branching. It is a relatively fast grower and should reach 6 feet within five years. American hornbeam, usually grown as a tree, grows more slowly.

Beeches (*Fagus* spp.), while most often regarded as trees, can also be used for hedging. Like hornbeams, beeches retain their leaves during the winter but the leaves of American beech (*F. grandifolia*) are much larger than those of European beech (*F. sylvatica*) or hornbeams. The American beech is hardy from zones 3–9, grows best in full sun, and is supposedly impervious to ice and snow; it is also more tolerant of cold and heat than European beech (hardy in zones 4–7). It needs good drainage, so plant on top of a low mound. Its growth rate is similar to that of hornbeams. European beech is said to tolerate a wider range of soils than American beech. Many old beech hedges in Europe grow to at least 12 feet, but they can also be grown as relatively short walls between garden rooms.

△ Their vibrant foliage makes blueberries an excellent alternative to burning bush.

△ The heavily veined foliage of *Carpinus betulus* 'Fastigiata' is lovely during all seasons.

◁ This bed between two driveways was planted with burning bushes that will have to be pruned into meatball shapes to keep them from encroaching on the driveways.

Spiraea is a genus of many species and cultivars. The leaves can be green or yellow, the flowers pink or white, and the height anywhere from 18 inches to 5 feet—and many also have excellent fall color. Spireas should be grown in full sun and well-drained soil. Most are fairly drought tolerant as well as cold and heat tolerant (zones 3–4 to 8–9).

Viburnum is another genus with several species and cultivars. It has lovely white flowers in spring, some very fragrant, and rose to maroon fall foliage. The only difficulty with viburnums is the appearance of the viburnum beetle, which decimates the foliage of some species. Consult with an extension agent in your area about which species seem to be less attractive to these pests. Viburnums can be hardy from zones 2–9 and grown in wet or dry soil and either sun or shade, depending on the species.

Fothergillas, depending on species and cultivar, can grow between 3 and 10 feet tall. They have white, bottle-brush-like spikes in early spring before the foliage appears and good fall color, particularly in full sun. Fothergillas are hardy in zones 5–9 and prefer moist soil.

There are of course many other options for hedge plants. Ask your friends and neighbors for recommendations and do some research on which will work best in your region.

▽ One of the cultivars of *Fothergilla* ×*intermedia*, like 'Blue Shadow' (shown here), would make an excellent medium hedge while *Fothergilla major* would work as a tall one.

△ This viburnum was selected as a hedge because it is very dense, even in winter, screening a corner house from traffic at a busy intersection.

◁ Short European beech hedges are used as dividers between garden beds.

▽ This long, unsheared spirea hedge is tall enough to hide the neighbor's house.

Perennials

If you were not a gardener before you inherited your existing landscape, you will probably not be able to identify the perennials (ferns are included in this category for purposes of this book) that are already in place. It is an important step in assessing the state of your yard, however, so ask someone from a local garden club or botanical garden or a landscape designer who specializes in perennials to help you identify them. Unless your landscape was designed by a plant lover, your perennials are likely to be commonly available and quite possibly ones that either seed voluminously or spread aggressively, both maintenance nightmares. Only by determining what you are dealing with can you understand the degree of maintenance involved and whether the perennials you have are ones that you want to keep or replace.

Once you know which plants you have, take some time to assess how they're doing. Much of their performance will depend on whether they are getting enough light and moisture without too much competition from tree roots. If tree roots are a problem

△ *Geranium macrorrhizum* 'Variegatum' (left), *Smilacina racemosa* (back right), *Aquilegia vulgaris* (very front), and *Heuchera americana* 'Dale's Strain' (front right) thrive in dry shade with a variety of textures.

◁ False Solomon's seal (*Smilacina racemosa*), planted at the base of a large magnolia tree, leans toward the light; these plants will need to be supported to keep them back from the sidewalk.

▽ Two asters (*Symphyotrichum novae-angliae* 'Hella Lacy' in back and *S. oblongifolium* 'October Skies' in front) are shown here at two different heights; had I cut back 'Hella Lacy' in June, however, they would both be the same height.

◁ △ *Penstemon* 'Dark Towers' blooms in my garden from mid June until the beginning of July (left), while the colorful deadheads (right) retain interest well into fall.

on your property, look for species that cope best under trees, generally known as dry shade plants. I have grown many successfully in my region, but you will want to spend some time researching those that work best in yours.

If your perennials tend to lean in one direction or another, they are probably planted in partial shade and seeking sunlight. The best solution for this problem is to move them to a location that receives more sunlight. One of the greatest assets of perennials is the ease with which they can be transplanted. Just be sure to water them before digging and then again after replanting. If you have tall, fall-blooming perennials that are floppy and fall over, think about cutting them back by half in June. They will be bushier and shorter but will probably bloom one week later than normal. (Tracy DiSabato-Aust's *The Well-Tended Perennial Garden* is still the authority on perennial maintenance. I suggest giving it a look.)

A well-designed perennial garden can be in bloom for several months, depending on the zone in which you live. The trick is selecting plants that bloom in different months, as well as plants with extended interest because of seedheads or interesting fall foliage.

Then, too, there are perennials like heucheras that have color twelve months of the year. The range of colors is amazing and those hybrids with *Heuchera villosa* heritage

△ *Heuchera* cultivars (clockwise from top left) 'Dolce Black
Currant', 'Citronelle', 'Southern Comfort', and 'Georgia Peach'.

△ *Coreopsis verticillata* 'Route 66' can be sheared after each flush of bloom to encourage floriferous rebloom.

are also very tough and drought resistant, even when planted in sun. Other cultivars are better suited to partial shade.

While there are many lovely flowering perennials, a perennial garden does not have to depend on flowers alone, but can be an unfolding exhibition of foliage with varying heights and forms (creeping, erect, droopy, mounding, open, compact) as well as foliage colors and textures.

There are basically two types of perennials: clumpers and spreaders. Clumpers are polite; they increase in diameter very slowly and rarely invade their neighbors' space. Spreaders, on the other hand, have roots that seek new territory and quickly overcome their well-behaved cousins. Spreaders can be curtailed with your hands or with a shovel, but vigilance is essential. That said, if you have a lot of space to fill, spreaders will probably be welcome.

Observe your perennials to determine whether they are self-cleaning or require deadheading. If they need to be deadheaded, can they be cut back in broad sweeps (shearing) or does each stem need to be hand-pruned? The difference in time can be quite intimidating. For example, threadleaf tickseed (*Coreopsis verticillata*), a perennial with very narrow foliage on wiry stems and available in many colors, can be sheared, whereas large-flowered tickseed (*C. grandiflora*), with its broader foliage, looks best when each stem is deadheaded. As demands on my time increase and my back muscles grow increasingly achy, I find myself favoring cultivars of *C. verticillata*.

Plant color is another element of plant selection that can be very tricky; it helps to have an artistic or well-trained eye. Each basic color has many shades and tints. Take red, for instance: is it wine, maroon, ruby, cherry, crimson, scarlet, brick, or rust? Suppose combining reds and pinks is desired. Which shades of pink (blush, salmon, coral, clear, rose, fuchsia) will be compatible with rather than clash with the desired shades of red? It takes a practiced eye to discern these subtle differences. I once visited a public garden where I was sure the designer was color blind. Two red annuals were planted together: scarlet sage (*Salvia splendens*) with orange undertones and a petunia with blue undertones that made it look ruby red. The combination hurt my eyes. Spend some time training your eyes to perceive the subtle differences and apply that practice to your perennial selections.

What about size? Have the perennials in your garden been planted with all the short ones in front, all the medium ones in the middle, and all the tall ones in the back? If so, I'm sure you find that arrangement to be quite dull. Fortunately, perennials can be transplanted rather easily most of the time. You can vary the heights at the front of the border by planting something tall there (as long as you can see behind or through it), such as the reseeding tall verbena (*Verbena bonariensis*), which can be grown as an annual or perennial depending on your zone.

∧ This vignette is composed of a wide variety of foliage types: the large, smooth leaves of *Hosta plantaginea*, the large, variegated and puckered leaves of *Hosta sieboldiana* 'Frances Williams', the linear leaves of *Panicum virgatum* 'Rotstrahlbusch', the small leaves of *Origanum laevigatum* 'Herrenhausen', and the scalloped leaves of *Ajania pacifica*. All of these will bloom eventually, but in late spring the foliage is the show (although the grouping is enlivened by *Clematis* 'Aljonushka').

▷ Although *Verbena bonariensis* is 4 feet tall, its stems are so narrow that I treat it as a see-through plant and often let it seed into the foreground.

▷ There are several reds and pinks in my west hill, but the common undertone of the plants (*Sedum spectabile* 'Neon', *Rosa* Oso Easy Cherry Pie, *Heuchera* 'Georgia Peach', *Berberis thunbergii* 'Golden Ruby', *Hibiscus* 'Pinot Noir', *Allium* 'Millenium') is purple, ensuring that the colors do not clash.

Ornamental Grasses

If you have inherited ornamental grasses, you will again need to identify them. This grouping represents a vast array of plants (and I am including sedges and rushes here, even though they are technically different). Grasses range in height from a few inches to 12 feet; vary in color (from green, to blue, red, yellow, or variegated); have inflorescences that vary in size, color, and type; die back in winter or keep their color; live in sun or shade; and differ in maintenance care depending on the genus. Just like perennials, some are clumpers and some are spreaders.

Ornamental grasses have a timeless quality that makes them usable with any type of building, whether traditional or contemporary. They were, in fact, quite the rage during the Victorian Era. One of the greatest assets of grasses is their texture and nowhere is it more needed than in old landscapes of stiff evergreens or as contrast to very linear contemporary homes.

Because ornamental grasses change in character with the seasons, they can add interest to an otherwise static landscape. In cold climates, the presence of the grasses during winter reminds us that the landscape is merely dormant, not dead, and when they blow in the wind, they are truly spectacular.

On the other hand, digging out any grasses that you don't like will be a chore of monumental proportion. The fibrous roots of most grasses are extremely strong and dense. When I have transplanted grasses, the pickax and strong helpers have been my

▽ The walls and driveway of this contemporary house are greatly softened by the loose texture of the grasses planted along the perimeter.

▷ Coming out of a conference one winter, I found myself in the middle of a snowstorm with *Miscanthus sinensis* blowing wildly in the wind.

△ Here, one pennisetum, blown by the wind, appears larger than it is.

◁ There are so many clumps of fountain grass (*Pennisetum alopecuroides* 'Hameln') planted together here that you see them as a mass rather than as individual plants.

most valuable tools. The alternative is selecting other plants, probably perennials, that grow nearly as high as the grasses you dislike; the new plants can lessen the impact of the grasses by hiding them.

Think about how the grasses in your landscape are used. Do you have one as a focal point or does the one look lonely? You can always add more, but before doing so, think about the type of look you hope to achieve. Normally, you space grasses as far apart as they are tall. This spacing enhances their massed effect, giving the appearance of an ocean of grass. Wider spacing will emphasize their individual character. Some grasses, such as feather reed grass (*Calamagrostis* ×*acutiflora* 'Karl Foerster'), which has extremely vertical inflorescences, will make a stronger statement with closer spacing to accentuate their verticality.

To vary layering in a bed, try using an ornamental grass with a delicate inflorescence as a see-through plant and place it at the front of the bed. I love to use purple moor grass (*Molinia caerulea* subsp. *arundinacea* 'Skyracer') this way. It has 2-foot foliage but 7- to 8-foot wispy inflorescences.

Grasses can also be used as screens or hedges. Those used as screens, of course, will need to be tall. Try giant reed (*Arundo donax*), which looks like corn on steroids, maiden grass (*Miscanthus sinensis*) if it is not invasive in your area, or our native switch grass (*Panicum virgatum*). Giant reed will grow 12 feet tall while the other two grasses have cultivars that will grow 6–8 feet tall. Hedges can be any height you wish, but they are typically 3–6 feet tall. A 3-foot-high hedge could be composed of fountain grass (*Pennisetum alopecuroides*), though this can be invasive in some areas. Red switch grass (*Panicum virgatum* 'Rotstrahlbusch') would make a nice 4-foot hedge. For a 4- to 5-foot hedge,

△ **The verticality of** *Calamagrostis* ×*acutiflora* **'Karl Foerster',** **in bloom from early summer until late fall, provides an excellent background for the more ephemeral** *Perovskia atriplicifolia* **in front of it.**

△ The thin inflorescences of *Molinia caerulea* subsp. *arundinacea* 'Skyracer' enable one to easily see the perennials behind it.

▷ The tiny blossoms of Siberian squill (*Scilla siberica*) peek out from the uncut grasses as a reminder that a chore has not been done soon enough.

try *Miscanthus sinensis* 'Adagio'. The beauty of this plant is its capacity to absorb being beaten down by heavy rain or snow and still become upright again. There are two drawbacks to using these grasses as screens or hedges. One is that the view beyond will be visible until the new growth matures and the other is the necessity of scything them down each spring. However, this is a lot less maintenance that most other types of hedges require.

You should also consider whether your grasses are positioned so that they are getting the best effects from sunlight. Inflorescences that are backlit become translucent rather than opaque. Foliage that is backlit can become translucent too, turning from red to flame, particularly in fall. And don't forget that frontlighting can also be used to create an appealing display. *Miscanthus sinensis*, in late fall, winter, or early spring before being cut down, is beige, but the early morning sun can turn it to burnished gold.

Maintenance of grasses is minimal. Most of them need only an annual scything in early spring before the new growth foliates. To mitigate the bare look just after scything, I plant bulbs between my grasses to partially hide them and also to fill the area with color. Timing is everything, so you need to know when to cut the grasses and which bulbs will bloom at or near that time. If you don't cut early enough, you will miss the blooms of the bulbs. In late spring, as the grass foliage emerges, it will hide the dying foliage of the bulbs. Evercolor grasses, like blue fescue (*Festuca* spp.) and blue oat grass (*Helictotrichon sempervirens*), stay blue all year and you need only comb through the foliage with your gloved fingers to remove the withered narrow foliage.

For the most part, grasses will suffer if you love them too much. Overwatering and fertilizing tend to make grasses lanky, so the word to remember here is "less." Happily, grasses mature relatively quickly, so newly planted ones look well established within a few years. Whenever you work with grasses, wear long sleeves and gloves because the leaf edges are like knives.

△ With the early morning sun shining on it, *Miscanthus sinensis* 'Adagio' becomes a gleaming mass of foliage.

Vines

Perhaps you have inherited some vines that are either growing up your house or on some other structure on your property. Of course, not all vines are welcome. Some vines like Boston ivy (*Parthenocissus tricuspidata*) and Virginia creeper (*Parthenocissus quinquefolia*) have outstanding fall color, but they can be very difficult to remove from walls without damaging the surface because the vines attach themselves with sticky, disklike appendages. Both of these vines easily grow 50 feet high. Another problem vine is the common ivy, *Hedera helix*, which supports itself with aerial roots that can penetrate cracks in stucco or the mortar between bricks. If you wish to remove them, gently pull the stems off the wall so as not to crack the mortar or damage the paint more than necessary. Use a wooden or plastic scraper to loosen any whole roots and stems that are still attached. The most time-consuming part of this job is using a dry nylon scrubber to get the tendrils and disks off the wall. You may need to turn to a stiffer brush and some water to get off the remaining remnants.

If you don't have any vines, perhaps you would like to add some. It is important to determine first how the vine will attach itself. I now have a series of wrought iron trellises along my fence but before I could afford them, I cut sections of chicken wire and attached it to my wood fence. I'm a clematis junkie and they need something to cling to with their tendrils.

Climbing hydrangea (*Hydrangea anomala* subsp. *petiolaris*) is a woody vine that attaches itself to almost any surface by twining and with aerial rootlets. Although best in part shade, I would recommend siting it in full morning sun to get the best out of the prolific white lacecap blooms. A vine similar in appearance but blooming earlier and longer is Japanese hydrangea vine (*Schizophragma hydrangeoides*). Cultivars include one that sports silvery leaves and another with pink flowers. Both of these vines are slow to establish but vigorous thereafter. They can also be a problem if grown up ornamental trees where they could shade out the tree foliage, thereby weakening it.

Most vines are best grown on support systems such as trellises and will need maintenance annually, if not more often. The most popular flowering vine is clematis, which is available in a wide range of colors, heights, size of bloom, and bloom times. Most people have no idea how to prune them and are afraid to attempt to do so. I think there is unnecessary mystification of the process because of the three pruning classification groups for different species and cultivars. Some clematis bloom on new wood only; others bloom on old *and* new wood—trying to remember which group each falls into will drive you crazy. To keep it simple, they all need to be pruned in spring just as the new leaf buds appear. And I let the vines tell me where to prune. I prune the deadwood (the part of the vine above the last foliating bud) unless I want to shorten the vine. That, however, is rarely the case; I want the vines to grow as tall as possible, usually about 10–12 feet, in order to reach the top of my fence. There are now some dwarf (3–5 feet tall) cultivars bred by Raymond Evison specifically for containers.

◁ I inherited this Boston ivy (*Parthenocissus tricuspidata*) that creates quite a splash of color on my fence where it can't do any damage.

▽ This climbing hydrangea will eventually cover the wall. At some point, (artistic) pruning will be needed.

Sweet autumn clematis (*Clematis terniflora*) is the one clematis I prune back almost to the ground because it would take over the world if given half a chance. It is quite beautiful in bloom but is very aggressive and seeds everywhere. There are two other species of fall-blooming clematis, both of which have yellow flowers and are better behaved. Raymond Evison's *Making the Most of Clematis*, despite being published in 1998, is still the best reference for pruning clematis that I have in my library.

If you have any wisteria on your property, it is likely that it is a common Asian wisteria (*Wisteria floribunda* or *W. sinensis*) with large bluish-purple panicles, spectacular blooms, and attractive divided foliage. Unlike clematis, which has green stems, wisteria is a woody vine. You should, however, closely examine the support on which your wisteria is growing. You want it to be constructed of a very strong material. If the wisteria is growing up the side of your house and into your gutters, be aware that it will eventually pull off the gutters. If the wisteria is not in bloom, you may want to prune it severely so that the plant's energy is diverted from producing more foliage. There are several cultivars of American wisteria, such as 'Amethyst Falls' and 'Longwood Purple', as well as cultivars of Kentucky wisteria, such as 'Aunt Dee', 'Blue Moon', and 'Clara Mack', that have shorter racemes (flower clusters); however, they are not as aggressive as Asian wisteria and bloom later, thus avoiding the problem of bud kill by late frost.

If you have trumpet vine (*Campsis radicans*), you might be wondering how to restrain it. It is extremely vigorous and can easily pull down a fence. It also suckers and seeds. Prune it hard annually in early spring; it will still put on a show if growing in partial to full sun. A similar vine, seen more in the southern United States, is cross vine (*Bignonia capreolata*), but it blooms in late spring while trumpet vine blooms in midsummer.

▷ Although *Clematis* 'Bill MacKenzie' is not as well known as many other clematis, it has a distinctive form and color and prolific bloom.

△ A brick pillar pro-
vides support for this
blooming wisteria.

◁ *Clematis terniflora*,
sometimes still sold
as *C. paniculata*, is
growing here on wires
strung between steel
posts and acts as a
property line divider.

Bulbs

Consider yourself lucky if the previous owner of your property planted bulbs to supplement the other plants in your landscape, or perhaps you were smart enough to do so yourself when you first started working in the yard. If you live in cold or temperate areas, the array of spring-flowering bulbs is quite wide. Many multiply and bloom year after year. If yours seem to produce leaves but no blooms, they may be too crowded or may not be getting enough sun. The best time to dig and separate them is immediately after the foliage turns yellow; at that point, they are going dormant. Some can be replanted in the original location and the rest can be planted wherever you see fit. Add a balanced fertilizer at the bottom of the hole and mix it with some of the existing soil. Then add a thin layer of soil before putting the bulbs in. (Do not use bone meal; it is not a complete fertilizer and seems to attract skunks and raccoons.) Since the area in which I live has heavy clay soil, I also add some enlarged aggregate at the bottom of the hole in order to increase drainage; bulbs tend to rot in wet soil. The best they can do is survive, but certainly not multiply. The large-flowered hybrid tulips do not rebloom well except in sandy soil, although some of the smaller species do. They are native to well-drained mountainous terrain that is dry during the summer.

If you live in the hotter climates of the southern or western United States, your choices for spring-flowering bulbs are more limited. Many of them, particularly tulips, need a period of cold to trigger the bloom process. On the bright side, many summer-flowering bulbs will be perennial in these conditions.

Don't forget that there are also long-lived bulbs that bloom in fall. Autumn crocus (*Colchicum autumnale*) look like huge crocuses. Their large foliage does not emerge until spring and goes dormant in late spring. Then in fall they seem to pop up out of nowhere. The name large autumn crocus is a misnomer for *Crocus speciosus* because they are much smaller than *Colchicum autumnale*. The other fall-blooming crocus is saffron crocus, *Crocus sativus*. All of these are fun to use in the garden because their blooms come as such a surprise.

There are two techniques for planting bulbs. The most laborious is digging individual holes for each bulb with a hori (Japanese digging knife) or trowel. I recommend the hori for its ergonomic design that puts less stress on the elbow and wrist. I often use this technique for larger bulbs like daffodils and tulips because I interplant them among perennials and grasses. For smaller bulbs (that I plant by the hundreds), use a shovel to dig large holes that can hold at least ten small bulbs or three large ones with space between to allow for future multiplication.

▽ The flowers of *Colchicum autumnale* pop up through any existing foliage.

Lawns

Many homes, of course, have almost no landscape; the default is lawn surrounded with a narrow bed of unattractive shrubs. Perhaps that is what you're dealing with now, but there's no better time than the present to do something about it. Less grass and more planting beds would provide greater visual interest and would improve the proportional balance between home and landscape, making the property look fuller, richer, and more balanced. The house should not dominate the landscape. Instead, as Gordon Hayward, a Vermont landscape designer and writer says: "Houses should be in, rather than on, the landscape."

Lawn, also referred to as turf, does not offer habitat or any benefit to the ecosystem. Since residential development, as well as industrial and business development, has fragmented our ecosystems, it is important that we try to restore habitat in the process of reinventing our landscapes. The typical, informal front yard is a large swath of lawn, a few trees, and, perhaps, a bed or two full of groundcover. One that creates habitat will have large beds of shrubs, perennials, and ornamental grasses, as well as groves of trees.

Another problem with most traditional lawns is that they are water guzzlers. Granted, there are some turf grasses like buffalo grass (*Buchloe dactyloides*) and no-mow grass (a blend of creeping fescues that interlock with bunch-forming fescues) that require less water, but they have not yet gained favor with most people, though they are gaining in popularity in the western and southwestern United States as a result of increasing drought. The reason such grasses are rarely used, at least in other areas, is that they do not remain green during winter. Some states that face water-supply problems are even debating legislative measures that would restrict the amount of lawn that a property can have.

◁ In the first spring after the lawn was removed, these immature plantings for part shade still provide more color and interest than the lawn did.

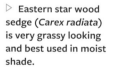 *Mazus reptans* does not look like grass but is an excellent ground-cover for large areas that do not bear much foot traffic.

▷ Eastern star wood sedge (*Carex radiata*) is very grassy looking and best used in moist shade.

There is also great concern over the amount of energy we consume in mowing our lawns and the air pollution that is created as a result. Very few of us are using the old push reel mowers anymore (nor are we receiving the physical benefits of the exercise that could be had from pushing those mowers around). Gas and electric mowers are a staple of the modern home. And if the property is large enough, the mower has morphed into a riding mower that consumes even more gasoline and requires almost no expenditure of calories. If you hire a lawn service, be aware that few services base their practices on the use of organics. Most utilize an array of herbicides and pesticides that end up in our water systems, contributing to water pollution and the growth of algae in our lakes and ponds.

Healthy lawns begin with good soil, choosing the right type of grass for your region and the amount of light your garden will receive, and aeration, which allows air, water, and nutrients to reach turf roots. The soil should be rich in organic matter and nutrients. Keep rototilling or excessive cultivation to a minimum because these processes can multiply weeds by bringing buried seeds to the top layer of soil where most weed seeds germinate. These techniques further increase weed problems by chopping weed roots into tiny pieces that will probably regenerate as new plants.

Mowing your lawn at the proper height will also keep it healthy. That proper height will depend on the type of grass you have. If you have to water, the best time to do so is between 6:00 and 10:00 am. Again, the amount of water (generally 1–1½ inches of water each week), will vary based on where you live and what type of soil you have.

Additionally, lawns are often set in partial shade, thus creating a never-ending struggle. One client I worked with had a very shady front lawn and desperately wanted to get rid of it. What I designed for him was a curving stone walk to the front door from the driveway. There was a large tree left of the walk and that area was extremely shady. We filled it with ferns, hostas, shade-loving wildflowers like variegated Solomon's seal (*Polygonatum odoratum* 'Variegatum'), and dry shade–loving shrubs. The right side of the walk was a bit sunnier, so there we added primrose, false forget-me-nots (*Brunnera macrophylla*), and Japanese kerria (*Kerria japonica*). Unfortunately, the garden had only just started to mature when my client was forced to move. The new owner moved in and promptly tore out the garden and tried to re-establish the lawn.

The reality, however, is that many of us like having some space for a lawn. The question to ask yourself then is: how much lawn do I really need? What is its purpose? Families need space where their children and dogs can play, but spend some time thinking about how much space you might actually need. One of the few benefits of lawns is that, from a design perspective, they can act as a visual balance to planted spaces or to hardscaping because they are relatively low and uniform, thus providing a rest for the eyes. But instead of grass, there are innumerable groundcovers—some of them grass look-alikes, such as lily turf (*Liriope* spp.) and sedges (*Carex* spp.)—that could fill this role; remember, however, that many of these are best suited to partial shade. If grown in sun, they are liable to look bedraggled at winter's end, so I suggest an early spring haircut. Such groundcovers could be a blessing since partial shade presents very difficult conditions for growing grass. They can be mowed occasionally but don't need to be. Contrary to popular belief, lawns do not have to be perfect. Why can't they be full of clover or creeping veronica that has tiny blue flowers in early summer?

If your property has grass-planted slopes that are very difficult to mow, this is likely because it was initially cheaper to seed the hillside than plant it with groundcover or spreading shrubs. In the long run, however, the maintenance costs of labor, equipment, and power will be higher. Seeing grass on steep slopes drives me crazy. I once did some maintenance in a client's perennial bed as the mowing crew arrived after a few days of rain. This property had a large turf area used as a lacrosse field, but the beds around it were above and on slopes. The large riding mower created a swath of mud and ruts as it proceeded up the slopes. Instead, slopes can be terraced with beds, steps, landings, and paths. A grass slope creates many more problems than it solves.

Why not invest in low-growing shrubs, perennials, ornamental grasses, or groundcovers that are rhizomatous (have underground runners)? They will grow densely, their roots will stabilize the slope, and they will add beauty and interest to the landscape. If you choose grasses native to your area, they will be accustomed to the amount of rain and snow as well as the endemic insects and will thrive.

When thinking about lawn alternatives, keep in mind that familiarity creates a sense of comfort. Therefore, in the course of changing expectations of what defines beauty and serenity, our alternatives need to also appeal to the neighbors. If the alternative is beautiful, the neighbors will not lodge a protest with the zoning board. For instance, landscaper Rosalind Creasy's front yard in Portland has no lawn. Instead it

▷ Rosalind Creasy has designed her front yard as a beautiful and colorful display of edibles.

△ I have used shrubs, perennials, and grasses in
my east hill to stabilize it, along with rocks at the
bottom to prevent the soil from washing away.

◁ A hillside garden in Portland is
anchored by boulders and covered
with ornamental grasses and shrubs.

△ The curvilinear design of the beds and the lawn draw you forward in order to discover what lies around the far corner.

is filled mostly with fruits and vegetables, but also flowers, vines, shrubs, trellises, arbors, and fences. It is colorful, interesting, and edible while being an educational focal point of the neighborhood.

On the other hand, a homeowner in my suburb of many period homes took out all of his lawn and planted his version of a tall grass prairie. Frankly, it resembled a weed patch. The idea deserves merit, but the execution was appalling because he did not take into consideration the necessity of marrying a house to its surroundings. The tall grass prairie would have been quite fitting in a rural setting, but not here. It is important that we lead by example in our neighborhoods, so if you are going to do it, be sure to do it right.

Another aspect of lawn to be considered is its shape. Since lawns are generally installed simply as a default, very little thought has been given to their shapes; often your lawn might seem fairly shapeless. For a lawn to be visually arresting or to counterbalance the height of plants within surrounding beds, the shape needs to be distinct.

▷ This lawn serves as a very wide path between rectilinear beds.

△ Horizontally laid brick makes a neat separation between the lawn and *Pachysandra terminalis*.

This could be done with strong, sweeping curves, or the lawn could be very linear. If you are so inclined, you may be able to redraw the bed and lawn lines yourself. You could also consult with a landscape designer or landscape architect.

Edging is another issue that will need to be considered. Edging helps give definition to the separation between lawn and bed, but maintenance of edges can be very tedious and cumbersome. You either need to trench the surrounding beds so that grass does not grow into the beds (a weeding nightmare once it's there), or you need to create a barrier. Trenching with the correct spade is a never-ending task. Grass, by virtue of its stoloniferous nature (it spreads by runners), will be constantly impinging on the trench you created. The other problem is that unless you use a taut string to define the lawn line, it will rarely stay the same. If you do take this approach, be sure to toss any clods of grass that you pull into a wheelbarrow and then compost them or use them to fill in bare spaces in the lawn. Do not throw them into the beds, where they will grow and create even more maintenance work for you.

If you decide to install an edging barrier, be aware that most plastic or rubber barriers are higher than the lawn, meaning that the mowers will not be able to get close enough to fully mow the lawn. The unmown areas will have to be cut with a string trimmer. Most rubber barriers are also unattractive and often heave out of the ground, though steel barriers usually remain in the ground because they are well anchored. Many barriers also do not go deep enough. Boulder edges are not necessarily the answer either; frequently, the grass just grows under them and then into the beds.

The best barriers I have seen are mowing strips that enable the wheels of a mower to run right over the strip. This strip could be composed of bricks or cut stone on end or stones or pavers that are laid over a deep base of small particle gravel that has been compacted. I would use brick-like pavers rather than real bricks, which tend to break down faster. The paving material should be held in place by an edging restraint specifically made for this purpose; if properly installed, it will not show. Any material used for edging should have a long life and should complement the rest of the landscape.

Architecture, Color, and Movement in the Winter Landscape

Spring and summer are certainly the busiest and most exciting seasons for your plants, but there are many delights that can be found in the winter season. Obviously we have no control over the chilly weather and lack of sunlight, but at least we can control the amount of color and interest in our landscapes. Consider yours during the cold seasons: is there any color? What about movement and other elements that would catch the eye?

Frequently, the winter landscape can be improved with better maintenance of your existing plant material and through the addition of some new plants. Overgrown trees and shrubs can be thinned and pruned to emphasize their architecture and artistry. Hedges, which delineate beds, will be more effective bones if they are carefully clipped to control their aggrandizing tendencies. Consider incorporating trees and shrubs that have colored or exfoliating bark or ones with unusual structure that can be utilized as architectural tools. Although most conifers are green, there are many with blue, yellow, or variegated foliage as well as a variety of different textures.

Many trees and shrubs have bright berries. I always enjoy watching the robins in the crabapple outside my office window. They tend to feast there when snow is on the ground. They also eat the berries on my winterberry (*Ilex verticillata*). Don't limit your landscape to red berries. Species of beautyberry (*Callicarpa* spp.) have bright magenta purple berries, a very unusual color at any time of the year. For yellow fruits, try *Viburnum opulus* 'Xanthocarpum', *Ilex verticillata* 'Chrysocarpa', or *Malus* 'Excalibur', 'Holiday Gold', or 'Bob White'. White berries abound on *Ilex glabra* 'Leucocarpa', while gray ones occur on bayberry (*Myrica pensylvanica*).

◁ The best time to prune small trees or shrubs for architectural structure is in spring, just before or just as they are foliating.

▷ The fruits of beauty-berry are an unusual bright magenta.

▽ The colorful, exfoliating bark of paperbark maple (*Acer griseum*) is worthy of a painting, especially when backlit.

△ When winter comes and the deciduous shrubs and trees have shed their leaves, the blue of the fescues will color this contemporary landscape.

△ The pods of *Iris sibirica* won't take stage until late fall and winter when all of the other bloomers have lost their color.

The only perennials that should be cut to the ground after a heavy frost are those that are limp and those that have been blackened by frost. The rest lend presence and appeal. Some remain evergreen; some have imposing structure. Others have pods that can add winter interest. Some of my favorites for winter are sedums, which resemble sculptures, especially when covered with ice or snow, baptisias, with black pods on stiff stems, and Siberian iris (*Iris sibirica*), with its strong stems and seedpods held upright above the bronzy orange foliage.

Ornamental grasses are also great, as they retain their inflorescences for all or most of winter. Although the foliage of grasses is usually beige during winter, that of little bluestem (*Schizachyrium scoparium*) becomes bronze while blue fescue (*Festuca* spp.) and blue oat grass (*Helictotrichon sempervirens*) retain their blue color year round.

How to Put Your Plans into Action

WHEN IT COMES DOWN to actually getting started on the hard work of reinventing your landscape, it is crucial that you first think realistically and deeply about how you value your time in contrast to the amount of money that you want to invest in this project. Consider how else you would like to use your time and then determine where in that list you will fit landscaping. How much of a priority will it be? You will also want to be realistic about what you do or don't know about landscaping and consider your ability to interpret and follow instructions. If you are someone who breezes through instruction manuals, you are probably ready to do almost anything. If, on the other hand, you glaze over after the first two steps, you may want to consider working with professionals to get it all done.

By now, you will hopefully have established a list of goals and priorities. A bubble diagram (see opposite page) is a simple way to take that list of priorities and see where you can fit them into the landscape of your dreams. Draw a simulation of your front or back yard, or use photographs, and then lay trace paper on top. Try to decide where you would put the features you want. Make sure you allow enough space for each feature. They may not all fit, so you will then have to figure out how to rearrange the pieces. Also, consider the circulation and traffic patterns in your yard and make sure that there is room for entry and exit of your wheelbarrow or lawnmower. Once you are satisfied with your bubble diagram, use a new piece of trace paper and turn the bubbles into definitive lines, so that you can get started.

Removing and Replacing Plants and Hardscape

Some of my clients jump into plant removal without really having a plan as to how to proceed thereafter. They'll say, "I just couldn't stand it any longer. I hated those shrubs around the house and I've dug all of them out but now I don't know what to plant there." For many plantings, it is quite possible that all you need is muscle and a sharp shovel to dig them out. On the other hand, the roots may be so old and extensive that a small Bobcat or tree spade is needed to unearth or transplant shrubbery, ornamental grasses, or volunteer trees that might be useful in a different location.

If you have trees that are decaying or are distorted due to loss of branches from storms or disease, they will need to be removed. Some people take it upon themselves to remove

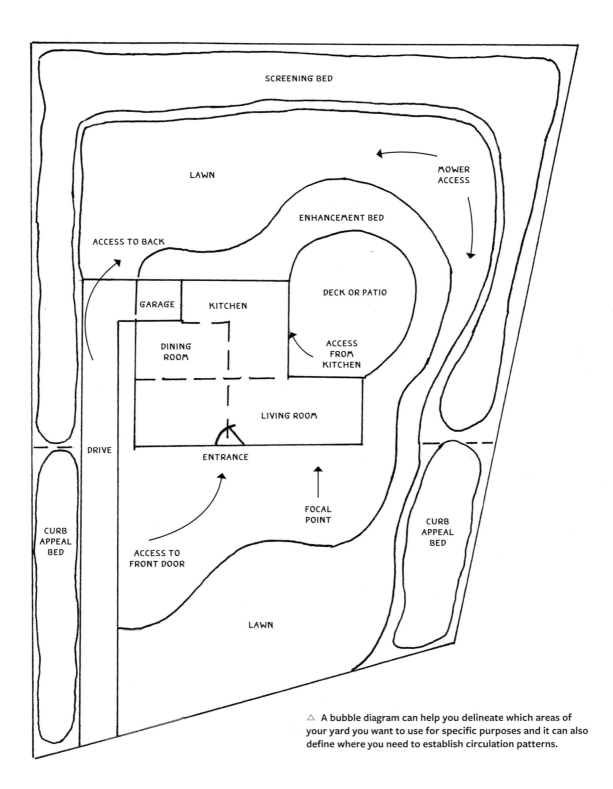

The labels within the diagram read:

SCREENING BED

LAWN

MOWER ACCESS

ENHANCEMENT BED

ACCESS TO BACK

GARAGE

KITCHEN

DECK OR PATIO

DINING ROOM

ACCESS FROM KITCHEN

DRIVE

LIVING ROOM

ENTRANCE

CURB APPEAL BED

ACCESS TO FRONT DOOR

FOCAL POINT

CURB APPEAL BED

LAWN

△ A bubble diagram can help you delineate which areas of your yard you want to use for specific purposes and it can also define where you need to establish circulation patterns.

△ It is impossible to see the trunk of this hawthorn because so many lower branches have been allowed to remain.

trees and stumps by themselves to save money but end up ruining their lawn and other landscaping in the process. Tree removal is a very demanding task; you risk injury to yourself and your property, maybe even to your house or your neighbor's, especially where there are large overhead wires. Arborists are not inexpensive but they have the expertise and equipment to handle these types of situations. They can also remove broken or diseased branches to prevent future accidents. If the ground below your trees is very shady and you would prefer more light there, arborists can thin the tree branches. The immediate expenses may be higher, but the long-term benefits are worth the cost.

You will also need to consider whether your municipality will pick up the vegetative waste from your tree removal or if there are rules about cutting the branches to a specific length and bundling them. You might need someone to haul it all away. Is any of it compostable? This is all hard, dirty, time-consuming work. The removal will leave holes in your soil that will need to be filled. This is another dirty job, but it will be easier if you purchase organic material in bags rather than in bulk. Bulk material is cheaper but you will have to shovel or pitchfork it into a wheelbarrow, trundle it to the site, and dump it. You also have to worry about distributing all of it into your beds before it rains or covering the pile and anchoring the cover so it is not blown off by wind. Carrying or barrowing bags to the site is much quicker. Again, all of these decisions involve questions of time vs. money.

If you only need a few bags, go to one of your local garden centers and purchase them there. If you want to buy a pallet of bags, usually forty to a pallet, look online for landscape-supply businesses that will deliver them to your house. The beauty of buying a pallet of bags is that you can store them and then use them as needed.

For removal of hardscape elements, it is again important to consider the work involved and the many different variables in the project before beginning the work. For instance, if the front walk is a straight line from the driveway to the door, but you want it to curve from the public sidewalk up to the door, you will need to remove the existing walk. What is that walk made of? Concrete, brick, or stone? Heavy stone slabs or smaller pieces that you can lever out and rearrange? If you think you might need more pieces to complete the job, where can you get them? You will also need to be prepared to construct a proper base so that the new or moved pieces don't rock or heave. If you're working with concrete, it will probably need to be jackhammered out. All of these questions will need to be answered regardless of the type of hardscape. For anything that seems beyond your abilities, do not be afraid to consult with a certified professional.

Soil Improvement

The world of soil can seem complex and intimidating, but soil improvement is an endeavor that almost any of us can handle with just a little research. Many, many books and treatises have been written on the subject. For years, it was believed that one must double dig the soil or rototill it to loosen it and then incorporate organic matter. The latest wisdom posits that rototilling destroys the web of micro-organisms in the soil and that we should lay soil amendments on top of the soil and they will work their way down into the soil with time.

The problem, however, is that most of us will not want to wait two or three years before planting. Therefore, I take a middle position. Loosen the soil with a spade or digging fork, lay the soil amendments on top of the soil, and then work them into the soil. It is a lot like making a soufflé. You fold the egg whites into the batter instead of stirring them in, thus lightening the batter but keeping as much air in it as possible. The same technique could be implemented here. As you plant, some of the soil amendments will automatically fall into the hole you have dug.

Loam is the term used to characterize the ideal soil, defined as rich and friable (crumbly), with nearly equal parts sand and silt, and somewhat less clay. But few of us have ideal soil. Yours may be heavy clay that doesn't drain well, mostly sand that drains too quickly, or very wet, even to the point of being boggy. Nevertheless, there are plants that are native to each of these types of habitats, and by making the appropriate plant choices, you will not have to amend your soil. For any plant selection you make, read up on its preferred conditions and decide whether or not it is appropriate for your soil.

On the other hand, if you want a landscape with plants that require good soil, you will probably need to amend your beds. You can purchase the best plants in the world but they will not thrive unless the appropriate soil is provided. So don't throw your money away. Start with the soil and then pick the plants. (See the Understanding Landscape Essentials chapter for advice on soil amendments.)

Adding New Plants

The first thing to consider when adding new plants is the size of the space that you are trying to fill. If you dug out a dead plant that was 6 feet wide, either select a replacement that will grow to 6 feet at maturity or two plants that will grow to 3 feet. The size of the plant when you purchase it will depend on availability and how patient or impatient you are when it comes to your garden. Generally speaking, small equals cheap. Larger plants will be more expensive because it takes longer to produce them but they will have more immediate impact when first planted. Unless you are able to purchase a mature plant, which is rare and expensive, new plants will generally look small and out of scale initially. Remember, they will grow. That said, even though they may be

▷ These fall-planted *Panicum virgatum* 'Northwind' and *Spiraea japonica* 'Gold-flame' looked small then but were selected because they would fill in quickly.

▷ The same plants, now much larger, are shown in June three years later.

Buying New Plants

The two main sources for new plants are garden centers and plant exchanges or sales. Most people garden, and shop for their gardens, in spring and early summer but stop when it gets hot in late summer or cold in fall. When shopping, remember that garden centers feature the plants that look good at that particular time. You should, therefore, shop more than once, perhaps seasonally. Keep in mind that garden centers stock what they believe will sell, so selection may be limited. If you are working with a professional landscape designer or landscape architect, they will have access to wholesale nurseries that grow many plants not carried by the garden centers. Such professionals will purchase wholesale and sell to you at retail prices. You will rarely pay more than at a garden center but you will have a much wider range of choices.

In many cities, there are horticultural societies, botanical gardens, and arboreta that have annual plant sales or exchanges. If you don't have plants to exchange, you can often purchase them for a small fee. The plant exchanges often have a pre-dominance of perennials that spread quickly, so be sure you know what you are buying. Neighbors or gardening friends can also be a plant source.

Inspect the plants carefully when shopping. Avoid those that are full of weeds, poorly pruned, or wilted. Plants should be well-branched; if they are leggy, they will stay leggy unless pruned to become bushy. These signs of neglect may be an indication that you should make your purchases at a different garden center.

If possible, carefully pull the plant out of the container and examine the roots that should be white or cream and not flat. If the plant has been in the pot for a very long time, it may be pot bound (meaning that the roots are tightly wrapped around the outer surface of the soil). In that case, you will need to carefully loosen the roots and spread them out before planting. In some instances, when the plant and the roots appear to be perfectly healthy but the roots are so entwined as to make loosening virtually impossible, I cut off the bottom inch of roots with a very sharp knife and then loosen the side roots.

very cheap, do not buy plants that are so small that you will lose all patience with your new landscape and grow frustrated. It is important to strike a balance.

At first glance, choosing new plants for a landscape might seem easy. You just go to a garden center and see what looks good. However, if that is your plan, you will be disappointed. Instead, be sure that you know how much light the site receives, how large you want the mature growth of the plant to be, whether you want a plant that is evergreen or deciduous, whether you want a plant that is interesting in more than one season, what type of foliage you want, what color flowers or berries you want, how long it will be in bloom, and what it will look like when it's not in bloom.

Assuming that you've only removed some of your pre-established plants, you will want the newly purchased plants to integrate well with what is already there. What type of foliage do the existing plants have? Keeping that in mind, then consider what types of foliage will contrast or blend well with them. Also, consider form. If existing plants are pyramidal, what type of shape will offer contrast: round, flowing, contorted, upright, linear?

If you are starting with a relatively empty landscape, plant the backbone plants first. These are the plants that give the landscape structure, mainly trees and hedges, because they take the longest to mature or grow together. The middle layer, usually shrubs and understory trees, comes next. Perennials and ornamental grasses should be last. They're the icing on the cake.

When planting, there are two things to keep in mind. First, make your planting holes larger than the size of the pot. There's an old saying that you should dig a five dollar hole for a fifty cent plant, meaning that the hole should be large enough for the roots to spread easily. If you amend the soil, mix some of the existing soil into the amendments so you don't create a hole that accumulates water. Be sure that you are installing the plant at the same level as it is in the pot. Second, if you are planting a tree, stake it (but not too tightly) for a year to give it time to establish its root system, which is, of course, its anchor. Remember to remove the stakes at the end of the year. Leaving them will inhibit healthy growth; trees need to move in the wind in order to develop strong trunks.

The ideal time to plant depends on where you live. That perfect time is when you can count on rain and the temperatures are cool to moderate. In the eastern and midwestern United States, this means spring ("April showers bring May flowers") or fall (until about mid-October). Conifers, in fact, need a slightly earlier start than hardwoods, preferring the warmer soil temperatures of summer to early fall. In the West, the rainy season is usually in fall and winter. Summer is the worst time to plant because high temperatures cause faster transpiration (evaporation of water through the leaves), necessitating more watering. Be aware, however, that some trees should not be planted in fall. Slow-to-establish genera are best planted in spring. These include bald cypress (*Taxodium distichum*), American hornbeam (*Carpinus caroliniana*), ginkgo, larch (*Larix* spp.), magnolia, hemlock (*Tsuga* spp.), sweet gum (*Liquidambar styraciflua*), tuliptree (*Liriodendron tulipfera*), and willow (*Salix* spp.). Also, broadleaved evergreens such as rhododendrons and narrow-leafed evergreens such as yews prefer spring planting. In general, plants with shallow, fibrous root systems can be planted more easily in fall than those with fewer, larger roots.

If rain is not reliable, you will have to water once every three days after planting. A deep watering at three-day intervals is infinitely preferable to shallow watering every day. You want plants to send their roots deeper into the soil to access water so that when they are on their own, they can withstand short periods of drought.

If you have planted in spring or summer, do not fertilize for the first year because the plants have been fertilized by the grower. If you plant in fall, you can also skip the fertilizer because you want to preclude the encouragement of new leaf growth at that time. In fall, what you do want to encourage is root adaptation and growth. If you plant in fall, allow at least two months of growing time before hard frost.

In early spring of the second year, just before new growth appears (do you see leaf buds forming on the stems?), you can lightly fertilize your gardens. I would recommend using an organic rather than inorganic fertilizer. The organics tend to be slow release and will, therefore, not be as likely to burn the roots. Another good time to fertilize is just after pruning flowering shrubs. Carefully dig the fertilizer into the soil so that it is not washed away by either rain or overhead irrigation.

Remember that your landscape is an outdoor extension of your home, and just as you would indoors, you need to make sure to keep up with your chores outside. As my friend and gardener Tracy DiSabato-Aust says, "Within a very short period of time, the garden of Eden becomes the garden from Hell unless regularly maintained." Never let your landscape go untended. Otherwise, you will have thrown away the time and money that you invested.

Working with Professionals

While there is certainly plenty that you can accomplish on your own when it comes to reinventing your landscape, sometimes limitations of time or knowledge lead us to seek out professional help. Would you build a house without having it designed by an architect? Think of your landscape as your outdoor house; why build it without a plan? You may decide to handle all the planning yourself, but if you think your project needs more expertise than you might have, consider how a landscape designer can help you. Landscape designers will be better able to translate your dreams into reality; they will be able to create functional yet beautiful outdoor living spaces. They will also be able

◁ Tile risers, that echo the pool tile, provide visual differentiation from the tread to alert the eyes to the approaching staircase—a great aide for the visually impaired.

to bring a fresh eye to your property, suggesting better use of space than you have envisioned, as well as find solutions to problems, some of which you might not even be aware of. Occasionally, partners will see the same space very differently, so meeting with a designer can provide an outside perspective.

Designers will have a greater knowledge of and access to plant material of which you may not be aware. If you let the designer know up front about the level of maintenance you want for your garden, he or she can choose plants that will conform with your goals. Even if you want a low-maintenance garden, an experienced designer will be able to enhance your property with seasonal interest, color, texture, and form.

A well-designed plan can save you from making mistakes and thus save you money in the long run. In addition, a designer will be able to explain how to implement the installation in phases and how to stay within your budget.

Furthermore, good designers will have the expertise to create or handle grade changes and make hardscape more accessible. For those of us in good health, it is difficult to plan ahead for a time when we're older and things might be physically more difficult. Patricia St. John, a friend and APLD colleague in San Francisco, never thought about these issues until she was injured and forced to use crutches. Her experience has opened my eyes and the eyes of our other colleagues. A good designer can also help you anticipate later concerns like loss of balance or diminishing eyesight.

LANDSCAPE DESIGNERS VS. LANDSCAPE ARCHITECTS

Landscape designers (LD) and architects (LA) are likely the two types of professionals with whom you will consult. The two fields are different in significant ways, however, and it is important to know which one you need. Sometimes a friend will introduce me as a landscape architect and I am quick to correct that misrepresentation. As a landscape designer, my training and skills are different from those of a landscape architect.

Landscape architects have university degrees in that field and are licensed by the state in which they practice. Their curriculum includes only one or two courses in botany—or sometimes none at all. They will have experience or training in aspects of civil and structural engineering, which enables them to work with elevation and grading problems (for example, steep slopes and retaining walls), as well as irrigation and drainage systems. An LA usually works on commercial or government projects, but some do specialize in large residential projects.

Landscape designers usually work on residential projects and are qualified through education, training, and professional experience to design landscapes. Many landscape designers are self-taught and have a vast knowledge of both plants and construction or they have two-year certificates from colleges, botanical gardens, or design schools. The

◁ **The step in the pathway here is indicated by the change in directional pattern of the bricks in the foreground.**

Association of Professional Landscape Designers (APLD) certifies qualified landscape designers who submit themselves and their projects to a certification process. Only those approved by the association can use the letters APLD after their names, just as only landscape architects who are licensed can use the letters LA after their names.

It is easy to quibble over these definitions. It all comes down to landscape planning, who is qualified to do it, and who suits yours needs and tastes. Both landscape architects and landscape designers are experts in planning the use of space and designing landscapes. Both want to preserve the environment and lately have emphasized making their designs as sustainable as possible. I would argue that landscape architects tend to have engineering education and skills that most designers do not, while landscape designers have a much deeper knowledge of horticulture. I also believe that landscape designers are more interested in aesthetics and enhancing experience with nature. While I have seen beautiful landscapes designed by landscape architects, I find that many of them are very formal and very sterile.

For those of you with serious grading or engineering issues, I recommend hiring a landscape architect. You could also hire both an LA and an LD, as one of my clients did. She had a steeply sloped backyard for which the LA designed several terraces and walkways; she then had me create all of the planting design.

HOW TO CHOOSE A DESIGNER

Before you start searching for the right designer (I am using the term *designer* generically here), make sure that you have established your goals and are able to articulate them. And once a plan is created, do you want your designer to carry it out, or do you plan on doing it yourself (it could also be a collaboration)? Be prepared to show the potential designer pictures from websites, magazines, or books that reflect your preferences and dreams.

Once you've done your preparation, don't just choose any designer at random. Ask your friends and relatives for recommendations. If you see any designed landscapes in your neighborhood that you like, ask your neighbors who they used and how the experience was. Visit the websites of recommended designers to learn more about them and see other projects that they have designed and installed. Check online reviews and ask questions. Does that company have the expertise to do the installation or have subcontractors on which it can rely? What materials and equipment might be needed? What precautions are taken to prevent damage to the lawn or other beds? Depending on the work to be done, is the company appropriately licensed, bonded, and insured? If the company website does not show professional affiliations or certifications, be sure to ask about them when you make an appointment to meet.

Keep in mind that while some companies offer free consultations, others charge and may or may not deduct the fee from the job price if hired. Designers from large companies are more likely to deduct the initial consultation than designers with small firms.

However, with a large company, you may not be working with the same person at all times.

Once you start meeting with prospective designers, there will hopefully be one with whom you click. Is the designer really listening so that the design will be personalized to reflect your own individual style? A complaint I frequently hear from new clients is that their prior designer(s) didn't really take the time to listen and the results were not what the clients wanted. My own high-maintenance landscape is a function of my obsession with plants, but I do not design that way for my clients unless they are also plant nerds and have requested such a landscape. Before you meet, you could ask the designer if the company has done projects similar to what you are looking for and ask them to bring photos of those projects to your first meeting.

If you are meeting with multiple companies, do not let price be the only factor that guides your decision. Designers are only human; they have varying degrees of creativity, passion, knowledge of design principles, communication skills, and experience.

Once you make a decision, it is crucial to have your designer come to your home so that the entirety of your space can be absorbed, including the views into your neighbors' spaces, as well as seeing your interior colors and design. Showing the designer photos in your meetings will not be sufficient. A design or advice on a design that will unify inside and outside can only be created once the designer is aware of all these factors.

THE DESIGN PROCESS

If you are interested in working with a landscape designer, be sure to factor the costs into your decision. Most designers base their fee on an hourly rate. Start with a consultation, in most instances one hour, during which time you should articulate your goals, and the designer will ask you a lot of questions while analyzing and assessing your site in order to identify all the essential conditions that will influence the design. This inventory includes the topography; existing hardscape elements such as walkways, fences, patios, and so on; offsite conditions; availability and quality of light, soil, moisture, and wind; and existing plant material. Be sure to discuss your budget. This is a good time to evaluate your personal compatibility with the designer. Assuming that you want to continue the relationship, the designer will then send you a design contract that outlines the probable cost of the design, outlines the steps involved, and asks for a design deposit to ensure your commitment to the project.

Once the design is complete, you must decide if you want the designer to act as your general contractor. If so, you can expect to pay an hourly rate for the designer's time to order your materials and plants, arrange for delivery, work with the subcontractors, manage the installation, and review the work in progress and at completion. If you will be acting as your own contractor, use the designer as a resource for other professionals who can help you implement the design.

After the contract is signed, the designer will return to your site to take measurements, which then lead to the creation of a base map (a bird's-eye view of your property, drawn to scale, showing the outline of the house and existing elements such as large trees and hardscape that will be kept).

Once the base map is created, the designer will use her analysis of the site conditions and your goals to create a conceptual design that takes both into account. Such a design or sketch will probably show where an offsite view needs to be screened or where there is one that should be used to advantage, where topography should or could be altered, and where circulation patterns are or should be. At this point, there should be a short meeting between you and the designer to ensure that you are both on the same page.

Then the designer will create two or three preliminary concepts based on different themes and arrangement of elements. These concepts may be supplemented with elevation sketches so that the designer's intent is easier to understand. Your feedback here will be crucial.

Based on the preliminary concept you prefer or by combining parts of each concept, the designer will then proceed to the creation of a preliminary design that will include grading, placement of hardscaping elements, and a planting plan. When that is complete, the designer will meet with you again for your feedback. Hopefully, she will bring pictures of the materials and plants she has in mind.

Once you have approved the preliminary design, the designer will convert it to final copy that should include a plant chart with the following information: botanical name, common name, quantity, mature size, bloom time, bloom color, and maintenance comments. If the plan is going out to bid, it should also include the desired installation size of the plants. The designer should also present you with an estimate for installation, broken into phases if you have previously indicated that you will not be able to implement the plan all at once.

Again, while working with a professional designer isn't necessary for everyone, as a certified landscape designer I can certainly vouch for the many benefits of hiring one to help you plan the reinvention of your landscape. I truly believe that it will be money well spent.

Success Stories

Some of the most satisfying aspects of being a landscape designer are seeing a design come to life, having happy and satisfied clients, and then staying in touch with those clients to watch the landscapes mature and modify them as needed. With three exceptions, the success stories that follow are the designs of my company.

Front Yards

A SUNNY DRY FRONT YARD

One of my very early clients was a single woman living in a ranch-style home in a Cleveland suburb. The first words she said to me were, "Please make the landscaping so beautiful that no one will look at the house." In our initial consultation, she told me that she loves orange, purple, and hot pink—no wimpy colors for her. She also told me that she particularly liked serviceberry (*Amelanchier* spp.) and pampas grass. I advised her that pampas grass would not be hardy in Cleveland, but instead we could substitute maiden grass (*Miscanthus* spp.). (The horticultural world has since learned that maiden grass can be invasive. Had I done this project recently, I would have used one of the tall switch grasses.)

△ The state of the front yard when I visited for the initial consultation.

There was some existing lawn and badly pruned evergreens that the client no longer wanted. I was told that I could take out as much of the lawn as I desired because she was spending too much time and energy dealing with it. On the right edge were railroad ties that she hated; she wanted them replaced with a stone edging and a defining line of shrubs. Although the house is very linear, my design was intentionally curvilinear in order to satisfy my client's request for that type of design and also to pull the eye away from the house. I kept her sidewalk but used two-thirds of the lawn for undulating beds. If the budget had allowed, I would have reconfigured the sidewalk as well.

The site had heavy clay soil that we amended extensively with leaf humus. It received strong sunlight for most of the day and had a slight slope.

My goal was to create a landscape that would be constantly changing, always interesting, and low maintenance. I created large sweeping beds that left only enough lawn to provide a visual contrast to the colorful plantings. I utilized flowering shrubs and perennials to give the client as much color as possible while also using some evergreens and ornamental grasses for winter color. On the right side of the house, there is a narrow bed between the house and the driveway. This bed is shaded by trees on the neighbor's property.

I have worked with this client for thirty years. Landscapes are not static and this design was merely a beginning that has been tweaked as circumstances have changed.

▷ **This is the front yard as it has evolved over the years. Most of the plants are the same, including the serviceberry and maiden grass.**

◁ The addition of *Heuchera* 'Southern Comfort' (right front) provides additional color on gray days and during the winter. It is amazingly sun and drought tolerant.

A SHADY DRY FRONT YARD

My first house had a front yard lawn that was totally shaded by three huge oak trees, each of which was surrounded with large circles of trees, and each of those surrounded by large circles of pachysandra. The rest of the front yard was lawn that was sparse at best. Trying to keep the lawn looking decent was an exercise in futility; however, everyone else on the block had lawn in the front yard so I felt compelled to retain it.

Eventually, tired of beating my head against the proverbial "wall," I vowed to take out all of the lawn as soon as I could afford to. Even though I had little plant knowledge and virtually no design experience, I started designing in my head with the intent of eventually removing all the grass and installing winding brick paths that would separate yet-to-be made beds from the pachysandra. The curvilinear design was dictated by the existing shape of the pachysandra beds. I would fill those beds with shade-loving perennials, ornamental grasses, and shrubs. By the time I could afford to implement my ideas, I had learned enough to choose drought- and shade-tolerant plants that would have a diversity of textures, forms, and bloom times.

Although that redesign took place over 30 years ago, the subsequent owners have kept the design and other homeowners nearby have attempted to imitate it. I am proud to say that this project was an award winner.

▽ **Winding brick paths, constructed with scavenged bricks, outline the curvilinear beds.**

△ This design for a front yard shaded by three huge oak trees has remained in place with very few changes for over 30 years.

A PARTIAL SHADE, MOIST FRONT YARD

The owners of this property lived just around the corner from my current house. They entertained frequently and came to me asking for a transformation of their front yard from a boring, green space to one that would be attractive and interesting year round, but with relatively little maintenance. (They were, however, happy and willing to have my crew come once a month to weed, prune, and deadhead.) They were also tired of mowing the slope across the part of the yard closest to the public sidewalk.

We decided to keep the large holly by their front door along with the other existing trees. Their color preferences were blue, pink, and white. The site faces east and has irrigation. The existing walk to the front door was an arc of stone that they wished to keep. Consequently, the entire design is curvilinear. The clay soil was heavily amended with leaf humus before planting.

I selected the plants for their variety of form and height as well as their ability to thrive in partial shade and slightly moist soil. Under the trees, I planted *Carex* 'Ice Dance', *Chasmanthium latifolium*, *Nepeta yunnanensis*, *Brunnera macrophylla* 'Jack Frost', ferns, *Astilbe chinensis*, *Geranium macrorrhizum*, *Campanula poscharskyana*, and *Actaea racemosa* (formerly classified as *Cimicifuga*). In the more open areas, I planted *Hydrangea quercifolia*, *Polygonatum odoratum* 'Variegatum' (variegated Solomon's seal), *Primula japonica* (that has seeded in beautifully), *Chelone lyonii* 'Hot Lips', *Cornus racemosa* 'Geauga', and a small maple.

On the slope, I used *Thujopsis dolabrata* 'Variegata', a woefully underknown and underused conifer, for its threadleaf and variegated foliage as well as its adaptability and its tendency to stay relatively small. I also added *Astilbe chinensis* 'Visions', *Lamium maculatum* 'Ghost', *Carex* 'Ice Dance', and *Heuchera* 'Georgia Peach'.

For evergreen color through winter and for textural contrast, there are also some yews, rhododendrons, and *Microbiota decussata*.

Five years later, the house was sold to another family, who have continued to retain my services. Since then, water problems in the basement necessitated digging up the middle of the main bed, but we were able to duplicate most of what was there before it was destroyed. We continue to tweak and maintain the landscape. Many naturalizing bulbs have been added in subsequent years in order to have color before the perennials bloom.

△ The front yard looking somewhat bare during the first spring after installation.

◁ In eight years, the shrubs have matured.

△ In spring, the hellebores and *Muscari armeniacum* (grape hyacinth) lend color to this bed beside the driveway.

△ In May, the bed right of the front door is ablaze with color as *Primula japonica* (candleabra primrose) comes into bloom.

△ *Heuchera* 'Georgia Peach' and *Muscari armeniacum* reflect spring colors elsewhere in the landscape. Within a few weeks, pink hyacinths will appear between the heucheras.

Back Yards

A SMALL PRAIRIE GARDEN

In the fall of 2012, I started working with a woman who loved to work in her garden. The south and west borders of her partially fenced back garden were dominated by a huge willow tree, which left that area of the garden frequently covered by shade. As the bed undulates north, there was a huge tree stump and several spindly, volunteer trees plus a number of undesirable groundcovers that were fighting each other for territory. The client, concerned for the health of her dog, was reluctant to use chemicals to kill the groundcovers. Taking a patient approach, we decided to use the technique of suffocation to kill off the plants. She saved newspapers throughout winter and in spring, after the tree stump had been ground out, we covered the bed with the paper, wet it down, covered it with an inch of the ground bark from the stump, and waited until late summer to plant.

▽ Before the redesign, the backyard view was of a partially bare fence, some yews, and the groundcovers.

This part of the garden is very sunny but moist, particularly in spring when you need waders to examine the garden closely. My client had complained that her garden was mostly a spring garden and she wanted to add a prairie garden. In this relatively small space, I designed for her a stylized prairie garden that will be most glorious in late summer and fall. I always preach patience, but it was really needed here. The first year after planting would have been a trial for anyone. The plants were still small and far apart. The second year, however, was a revelation. Most of the plants became huge, helped by prolific spring and early summer rains. By the third year, it was well established.

▽ In mid-spring, the prairie garden still looks fairly empty. The white and red flags denote spaces for plants that have not yet been installed.

▷ By mid-August, the garden is quite full and colorful.

△ The back yard before work begins: a small concrete patio leads out to a spotty strip of lawn (the orange paint marks out space for the new walk that will replace the lawn).

A SHADY BACK YARD REDESIGN

This project was completed for an older couple nearing retirement. The couple wanted a larger patio that would be more inviting than the existing concrete pad and an attractive transitional area that would connect the new patio to an existing deck. The transitional area would replace lawn that was not doing well due to a lack of steady sunlight. The designer, Jeff Nawrocki of Outdoor Concepts, chose to echo the diagonal design of the deck in order to unify all of the hardscape elements of the back yard.

The paving stone (a product called Unilock Rivenstone) was chosen by the client. Although lovely, it is thin, which meant that the contractor could not use his compactor because the vibrations would have cracked the stone. Rockfaced (weather-worn) sandstone was used to create the steps. In keeping with the stone theme, boulders were placed along bed edges to help retain the soil.

△ The diagonal design makes this back yard much more interesting, while the boulders continue the stone theme.

◁ The same paving stone is used for the path below the steps that leads to the back lawn.

▽ The diagonal design of the patio and the transition area echo the diagonal design of the existing deck.

EAST MEETS WEST: A SUNNY BACK YARD

This redesign by Patricia St. John, FAPLD, was completed on a property located in the San Francisco area. The flat backyard lot faced south and had a creek flowing beyond the back fence. The existing deck had a rickety, wooden, overhead structure. The back yard was divided by a low fence, with concrete beyond the deck and lawn in the other half. The region had recently experienced drought conditions, although it generally has a Mediterranean climate.

The client, born in Shanghai, China, wanted to redesign his ranch home to capture the modern, simple, understated elegance that he experienced growing up in China. He wanted a garden that would echo the interior aesthetic of his house and where he could entertain ten to twenty people at a time. He also wanted to seamlessly connect the outdoor space with the home. To this end, the interior designer was installing a 14-foot folding glass door to easily access and view the back yard from the dining and room area. Opening up the view of the creek was important, as it would expand the visual impact of the back yard. The area to the west of this space contained a gravel Zen garden, which had recently been installed to replace what was previously lawn.

Because the interior work would eat up most of the client's budget, he wanted the garden project to be relatively inexpensive. The client also wanted to reuse as many materials as possible from the present garden. These two desires fortunately went hand in hand. At the landscape designer's suggestion, the existing deck was dismantled, and the boards were flipped and then stained. The rebuilt deck used existing piers

▽ Before work begins, standing on the existing deck with railings all around and covered by an arbor, one feels hemmed in.

◁ The new deck feels expansive and relates well to the house. The sails shade the back deck and the back of the house.

▽ The reconfigured concrete patio is serene with its linear patterns and simple plantings.

and joists where possible. It connects to hardwood floors inside the house and the dining room table includes wheels so that it can be easily rolled out to the deck for summer entertaining. Posts from the old arbor were also retained. Together with new beams, they were strung with 5-foot-wide nylon sails that span a 25-foot expanse. The five nylon sails were relatively inexpensive and are retractable when more light is needed or when the portable fire pit is placed on the deck for evening entertaining. The deck lighting is LED outdoor lighting. Patricia's use of new, inexpensive materials helped meet the client's budget constraints while reflecting the modern garden aesthetic.

Rafters from the old arbor were reused to build steps creating access from the deck to the rest of the yard. The existing concrete was saw-cut into 3-foot-wide strips with a foot of space between that was filled with grasses and black La Paz rock as mulch. A small patch of new concrete was poured to continue the pattern of the new design. Expansion joint boards in the old concrete were left because they created an interesting abstract pattern.

The existing back fence was retained, but pairs of square 3-foot "windows" were cut out, framed, and set in wire for security. This opened up the view to the creek and outlying vegetation.

The plantings were simple: clumping bamboo used as a screen along the side fence, Berkeley sedge (*Carex divulsa*) in strips along the concrete, Cape thatching reed (*Elegia tectorum*) in random spaces, basket grass (*Lomandra longifolia*), an evergreen, and drought-tolerant grass along the back fence to echo the grasses beyond the fence. All were drought tolerant except the bamboo; and drip irrigation was used throughout the garden. Several ceramic balls were placed in the garden and pots were added to the deck to add punches of color. This was another award-winning design.

▽ The redesigned back fence provides security while opening the view from the deck to the borrowed scenery beyond.

Side Yards

Because most side yards are long and narrow, it is always a challenge to come up with an interesting design for that kind of space. In this case, the space became a room rather than a hallway. Cleveland designer Kevin O'Brien was once asked to create a side yard that would be interesting yet low maintenance. His solution was to use intersecting paths that had different textures, simple plantings, and a fence window that allows visitors to peek into the garden before entering it and also serves as a focal point when embarking on the return journey.

The gravel and pebble curvilinear path, on which one enters the garden, encourages the owner and visitors to wander slowly through this serene garden in order to appreciate the seemingly simple planting—which is actually an excellent and thoughtful mix of contrasting textures. The cut stone rectilinear path, centered on the bay window at the back of the garden, provides a visual line from the entry end of the garden to the bay window at the other end. This path actually stops at a hosta that is growing in the middle of an unusual, hollowed-out rock. Between the hosta and the bay window is a simple recirculating fountain that adds the element of sound.

This is a garden meant to be viewed from inside as well as outside. Therefore, none of the plantings in front of the bay window or the porch are tall enough to obstruct the view.

▽ Before hiring a landscape designer, the owner of this narrow side yard was stuck looking at grass that didn't want to grow and shallow, stone-covered beds.

△ The curvilinear gravel path now provides a visual means of making one forget that the site is long and narrow, while the rectilinear path provides firm footing.

▷ The path eventually stops at this hosta plant growing in the middle of a large, flat rock.

Entire Properties

A SINGLE-FAMILY HOME

This client lived alone in a charming house, but wanted a more welcoming front entry, an attractive and usable patio, and a better back-door entrance. As an older woman, she didn't want to juggle packages when standing on the steps to the back door. The rotting wooden steps had recently been replaced with concrete ones, but the tread was quite narrow.

The front walkway was a typical contractor's walk: a narrow, concrete L-shape from the driveway to the front door. We substituted a wider, large stone-like paver path edged with brick pavers that echo the brick in the framing of the windows and door of the house. We also made the area by the front steps large enough for a chair so that our client could sit there awaiting family and friends.

The back patio was unusable. The concrete pavers were crumbling and the contractor who replaced her steps left a gravel mess. The client was forced to put her patio furniture at the back of her driveway in order to have a stable floor. However, it meant that she could not enjoy the lovely plantings that existed on the side of the garage facing the

▽ Before the transformation, the front yard and the entrance to it were quite pedestrian.

△ The newly installed walk is both attractive and inviting.

house. Using the same materials as the front, we created a wide, curvilinear path from the driveway to the back door. The new step has a paver riser and a stone slab tread. The bed in front of the garage was deepened and most of the existing plants were retained, but in a different configuration. There is now a new paver patio so the client can sit between lovely plantings on all sides.

◁ The back patio and steps in their previous state were ugly and unsafe, and the lack of a stable patio forced the homeowner to resort to using her driveway as a makeshift patio.

▽ Now, however, the new back walk and patio invite one to come and have a seat.

△ Before redesign, the front yard was a sea of poor lawn, overgrown shrubs, and one lone tree.

A TWO-FAMILY HOME

My client for this project was a woman in her 60s with some physical disabilities as a result of a car accident. She lives in a suburb with many rental or two-family homes that have minimal landscaping. Her soil, typical for where she lived, was heavy clay that retains water and drains poorly. Also, the low soil level in her back yard needed to be raised. Her desire was for a drought-tolerant (xeriscapic), low-maintenance landscape, so it was necessary to amend the soil to create excellent drainage. The front of her house faces east and is unobstructed; the back faces west and has good light in the morning and full sun in the afternoon.

In a space that was stark, unusable, and a bit of an eyesore, I was asked to create a welcoming, colorful, ever-changing, usable landscape with minimal maintenance, lots of color, the use of ornamental grasses, removal of all turf, a reconfigured

▷ Now, in late spring, the front yard highlights are the blooms of *Sedum rupestre* 'Angelina' and *Euphorbia polychroma* 'Bonfire', along with the yellow foliage of *Spiraea* 'Dakota Gold-charm'.

◁ In early fall, the blue foliage of *Helictotrichon sempervirens* is still prominent, as are the blooms of *Perovskia atriplicifolia*, *Pennisetum alopecuroides*, and *Panicum virgatum* 'Northwind'.

▽ A few weeks later, the foliage of *Pennisetum alopecuroides* begins to assume its yellow fall color, while the *Hydrangea quercifolia* foliage turns maroon.

front walk, replacement of the back steps, and a relaxation and grill area in the back while utilizing as many existing site materials as possible.

This relatively small property, with no irrigation system, had the typical, narrow contractor front walk that was totally obscured by overgrown yews and a temporary back walk. Other than one existing tree, there was only poor turf in the front and on the tree lawn. The back was mostly bare soil and an assortment of junk and sawn logs (from a dead tree).

The front and back walks were reconfigured into wide sweeps. The front walk now allows unfettered access from either side of the property to the front door while journeying through the landscape.

In the back, the curvilinear theme of the front walk and the existing concrete driveway was continued with a wide sweeping walk to the back staircase to allow for easy conveyance of groceries and packages, as well as an arc and tangent patio, both poured in concrete. The dimensions of the patio were sized to those of a small canvas gazebo that the client had previously purchased. Although the back staircases, badly in need of replacement, were redesigned, budgetary constraints have left that work for the future. For now the back walk leads to what will eventually become the sole staircase. The design was created and implemented in the spring of 2008, and augmented with naturalizing, deer-resistant bulbs a year later. The client now loves to look out the windows, spend time on the patio, and welcome visitors.

To create a low-maintenance, deer-resistant, sustainable landscape, I selected plants that would be tough enough to withstand the vagaries of the region's weather—drought resistant yet wet tolerant for short periods of time—as well as varied in texture,

▽ The golden yellow foliage of *Amsonia hubrichtii* echoes that of the *Pennisetum alopecuroides* and the tree, while the orangey foliage of *Panicum virgatum* 'Northwind' acts as a backdrop.

◁ If perennials and grasses are not cut back in fall, their foliage and deadheads remain as sculptural elements in the landscape.

▽ The back yard, which had for several years been used as a junk yard, has been transformed. Only a year after installation, the client was able to enjoy the new back patio, tent, and plantings.

form, height, and season of interest. The plant palette I went with includes perennials, grasses, both deciduous and evergreen shrubs, and a few trees. Several genera are repeated in front and back in order to create a unified landscape. Some plants, such as the silver-stemmed Russian sage (*Perovskia atriplicifolia*), were chosen because their color echoes that of the house. The grasses are beautiful year round, particularly when blowing in the wind. Many of the chosen plants have beautiful fall color or bloom, such as bluestar (*Amsonia hubrichtii*), Russian sage, stonecrop (*Sedum rupestre* 'Angelina'), ninebark (*Physocarpus opulifolius* 'Diabolo'), and seven-son flower (*Heptacodium miconioides*). Although only drought-resistant plants were used, instead of looking like a desert landscape, the landscape retains a strong sense of place by featuring several plants that are commonly used in the region.

When the sod was stripped from the front yard, the grade was adjusted, with the excess soil being moved to the back. The soil was then amended with local leaf humus. A large boulder, unearthed during soil prep, was used as a focal point amid the bluestar in the front bed. After the plantings were installed, the landscape was mulched with either gravel or shredded bark, both from local sources, depending on the needs of the plants. The tree lawn was amended with gravel to facilitate drainage and the growth of a groundcover sedum. The chips from a tree stump were ground out and used to mulch a previously weedy area between the garage and the neighbor's garage. The new front walk is permeable, with existing stone from the back now set into gravel. Although the back walk and patio are concrete, the soil has been graded so that runoff flows to the back of the property where much of it is absorbed by the heavily mulched area between the garages. After the first year of establishment, little water has been used to maintain this xeric landscape. Habitat has been created where, formerly, there was none. This design, another award winner, is a neighborhood landmark.

◁ **The back area, as viewed from the garage, is replete with** *Panicum virgatum* **'Northwind', repeated from the front, sedum, and herbs.**

Bibliography

Adams, Denise Wiles, and Laura L. S. Burchfield. 2013. *American Home Landscapes: A Design Guide to Creating Period Garden Styles*. Portland, Oregon: Timber Press.

Avant Gardener. 2013. "Soil Science: Soil Microbes and Their Effect on Plant Growth." December.

Bennett, Pamela, and Maria Zampini. 2015. *Garden-pedia: An A-to-Z Guide to Gardening Terms*. Pittsburgh, Pennsylvania: St. Lynn's Press.

▷ In the process of writing this book, I have used many terms that have become second nature to me but might seem quite foreign to you. If that is the case, I highly recommend that you purchase and keep by your side this book written by two of my Ohio friends and colleagues. The book includes words and phrases that refer to aspects of landscaping as well as gardening and horticulture.

Brunet, Helen Tower. 1989. "Bambi Go Home." *The Green Scene*, January. Pennsylvania Horticultural Society.

Clausen, Ruth. 2011. *50 Beautiful Deer-Resistant Plants*. Portland, Oregon: Timber Press.

Creasy, Rosalind. 2010. *Edible Landscaping*. Portland, Oregon: Timber Press.

Darke, Rick, and Doug Tallamy. 2014. *The Living Landscape: Designing for Beauty and Biodiversity in the Home Garden*. Portland, Oregon: Timber Press.

Dirr, Michael. 2011. *Dirr's Encyclopedia of Trees and Shrubs*. Portland, Oregon: Timber Press.

DiSabato-Aust, Tracy. 1998. *The Well-Tended Perennial Garden: Planting and Pruning Techniques*. Portland, Oregon: Timber Press.

Dunnett, Nigel, and Noel Kingsbury. 2004. *Planting Green Roofs and Living Walls*. Portland, Oregon: Timber Press.

Evison, Raymond. 1991. *Making the Most of Clematis*, Second Edition. Wisbech, Cambs: Burrall Floraprint Ltd.

Garnham, Peter. 2014. "The Community Below Ground." *Horticulture*, March–April.

Hadden, Evelyn J. 2012. *Beautiful No-Mow-Yards*. Portland, Oregon: Timber Press.

Holmgren, David. 2002. *Permaculture: Principles and Pathways Beyond Sustainability*. Hepburn, Australia: Holmgren Design Services.

Messervy, Julie Moir. 2014. *Landscaping Ideas That Work*. Newtown, Connecticut: Taunton Press.

Owens-Pike, Douglas. 2014. *Beautifully Sustainable*. Minneapolis, Minnesota: Be-Mondo Publishing.

Sunset Magazine. 2012. *The New Sunset Western Garden Book*.

Tallamy, Douglas W. 2007. *Bringing Nature Home: How You Can Sustain Wildlife with Native Plants*. Portland, Oregon: Timber Press.

Thompson, Peter. 2007. *The Self-Sustaining Garden*. Portland, Oregon: Timber Press.

Zanon, Scott A. 2009. *Desirable Trees for the Midwest: 50 for the Home Landscape and Larger Properties*. Self-published.

———. 2014. *Landscaping with Trees in the Midwest: A Guide for Residential and Commercial Properties*. Athens: Ohio University Press / Swallow Press.

Online Resources

The following list includes many of the websites that I visited for information while writing this book. If you wish to delve more deeply into any of these resources, I have listed them by subject matter.

ACCESSIBILITY DESIGN

access-board.gov/guidelines-and-standards/recreation-facilities/guides/play-areas
Provides guidelines for play areas from the Americans with Disabilities Act (ADA).

ada.gov/2010ADAstandards_index.htm
Provides ADA standards for accessible design.

DECKING

www.whitecedar.com/Species.htm
Information on the benefits of using white cedar for decking.

weekesforest.com/products/decking-rail-and-fencing/
Information on the use of several different types of cedar for decking.

hgtvremodels.com/outdoors/plastic-vs-composite-decking
Explains the differences between plastic and composite decking.

consumerreports.org
A good source to compare ratings for decking materials.

EDIBLE GARDENING

apiosinstitute.org
Profiles and photos of more than 500 useful and edible plants.

FIRE PITS

avantgardendecor.com/blog/clean-a-fire-pit/
Fire pit cleaning and maintenance tips.

FIREWISE LANDSCAPING

forestry.ces.ncsu.edu/recreation-and-aesthetics/
Provides guidance in plant selection, placement, and maintenance tips for creating a "survivable space" extending at least 30 feet outward from your home in all directions.

GOOSE CONTROL

organicgardening.com/living/8-ways-deal-goose-invasion
Tips for dealing with geese.

HARDINESS ZONES

sunset.com/garden/climate-zones/climate-zones-intro-us-map
Other factors that Sunset *includes in calculating its hardiness zones.*

INVASIVE PLANTS

usna.usda.gov/Gardens/invasives.html
A good resource for information on common invasive plants in the United States.

IRRIGATION

asic.org
Website for the American Society of Irrigation Consultants.

irrigation.org
Website for the Irrigation Association.

turfdesignbuild.com/services/smarter-systems/
"Smarter Systems," an article by Tom Crain in the March 2014 issue of Turf Design Build, *offers a discussion of technological improvements to irrigation systems.*

LANDSCAPE EDGING

news.aces.illinois.edu/news/bed-edges-pull-landscaping-together
A great article by Rhonda Ferree on the benefits of edging.

LAWN

oregonlive.com/hg/index.ssf/2014/07/lawn_alternatives_green_up_you.html
This 18 July 2014 article by Kris Wetherbee in the Oregonian *offers suggestions on green alternatives (groundcovers) to turf.*

ORNAMENTAL GRASSES ON STEEP SLOPES

blogs.usda.gov/2014/09/15/usda-plant-experts-help-cemetery-tame-slope-with-native-grasses/
A useful article on managing slopes with ornamental grasses.

OUTDOOR PLAY

greenheartsinc.org/uploads/A_Parents__Guide_to_Nature_Play.pdf
An exposition on why and how to give your children more outdoor play with many suggestions on how to "kidscape" your yard and how to increase family play.

PERMEABLE PAVING

asphaltpavement.org/index.php?option=com_content&view=article&id=507&Itemid=1122
Points out the merits of using porous asphalt.

hardscapemagazine.com/complete_issues.php
In the February/March 2014 issue of Hardscape Magazine, *there is a great article by Tom Hatlen ("Pavers Designed for Drainage, and for Growing Business") that is full of information about the different types of permeable pavers and how crucial drainage is. While this website can be a little difficult to navigate, there is a wealth of information to be found.*

POOL DESIGN AND INSTALLATION

genesis3.com

A website for the National Swimming Pool Foundation, and a good place to search for a certified pool professional.

RACCOON CONTROL

humanesociety.org/animals/raccoons/tips/solving_problems_raccoon.html

Tips on what to do about racoons.

RAIN GARDENS

nrcs.usda.gov/wps/portal/nrcs/detail/ct/technical/ecoscience/?cid=nrcs142p2_011073

Guidelines for rain garden site and soil assessment.

RECYCLED GRANITE

RecycledGranite.com

Tips on the many ways in which discarded granite can be used.

REJUVENATION PRUNING

hort.purdue.edu/ext/ho-4.pdf

Information on pruning techniques for ornamental trees and shrubs; see page 9 in particular.

SHEET MULCHING

wildwillowdesign.com/2011/06/three-ways-to-sheet-mulch

Describes the advantages of sheet mulching, and provides three relatively easy ways to do it.

wmassmastergardeners.org/1111.htm

Describes how to use sheet mulching to create raised beds.

SOLARIZATION

ipm.ucdavis.edu/PMG/PESTNOTES/pn74145.html

"Soil Solarization for Garden & Landscapes." UC IPM Online. October 2008.

TREE PLANTING

treesaregood.com/treecare/resources/new_treeplanting.pdf

Tips for planting trees.

WEED CONTROL

grit.com/departments/natural-weed-control-zm0z13mjzgou

Another great article by Kris Wetherbee on natural weed control; it includes many tips for those who do not want to use herbicides in their gardens.

WILDLIFE HABITAT

nwf.org/Garden-For-Wildlife/Create.aspx

Information from the National Wildlife Federation on creating your own certified wildlife habitat.

Acknowledgments

To my many horticulture and landscape design friends in the green industry who have offered patient support throughout my career and during the completion of this book. To my former colleague, Bill Healy, a talented designer who is sorely missed, and to all the other authors who have offered advice and empathy. To my late mother, a strong woman who could have been CEO of any corporation if she had not dedicated herself to a philanthropic organization. To my friend Stephanie Cohen, a great roommate and the only person who makes me laugh more than my husband.

I would also like to offer my thanks to the following, who have designed with me, shared their photography, taken time to discuss and explain aspects of landscaping that are not my strong point, read drafts of the manuscript, and consistently inspired me: Steve Castorani (North Creek Nurseries), Bill Hendricks, June Huston (Missouri Botanical Garden), Ethan Johnson, Mary Jane Levin, Connie Modrak, Vanessa Nagel, Jeff and Lori Nawrocki, Jay and Tina Nyce, Kevin O'Brien, Patricia St. John, FAPLD, Connor Stedman (Appleseed Permaculture LLC), Kathy Stokes-Shaker, APLD, and Brian van Bouwer.

Photography Credits

All photographs are by the author, except for the following:

Alma Hecht, page 123 (top)
Bill Hendricks, pages 163, 169 (top left, right), 171 (top)
Reuben Huffman, page 131 (bottom)
Ethan Johnson, page 157 (top)
Missouri Botanical Garden, page 158 (bottom left)
Jeff Nawrocki, pages 228, 229
Jay Nyce, page 53 (bottom right)
North Creek Nurseries, page 190 (bottom)
Kevin O'Brien, pages 233, 234 (top)
Jason Reeves, page 104 (top)
Patricia St. John, pages 230, 231, 232
Linda Zolten Wood, page 47 (top)

Index

BOBBIE SCHWARTZ, FAPLD, is the owner of Bobbie's Green Thumb in Shaker Heights, Ohio. She has been an obsessed gardener for 48 years and a landscape designer for 40. Her landscape signature is the use of perennials, flowering shrubs, and ornamental grasses to facilitate color and interest throughout the year. She has been a member of both the Association of Professional Landscape Designers (APLD) and the Perennial Plant Association (PPA) since their inception and served twice as president of the APLD. She has won several awards for her designs, lectures nationally, and has written many articles on landscape design and the use of perennials. Her previous book, *The Design Puzzle: Putting the Pieces Together*, is a collection of articles about the elements of design and the use of plant material from a design point of view. Bobbie travels extensively to attend innumerable garden conferences and workshops, taking photographs of the many gardens that she visits and learns from along the way.